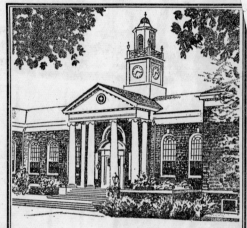

D1279140

KÄTHE KOLLWITZ

Life in Art

MINA C. KLEIN

H. ARTHUR KLEIN

KÄTHE KOLLWITZ
Life in Art

illustrated

Holt, Rinehart and Winston · New York · Chicago · San Francisco

    ISBN: 0–03–084208–5 (Paper)
    ISBN: 0–03–086362–7 (Trade)
Library of Congress Catalog Card Number: 72-150027
Printed in the United States of America
First Edition

Design by Lynn Braswell

To the youth who are working to achieve at last
the hope and demand of Käthe Kollwitz:
Nie Wieder Krieg! (Never Again War!)

CONTENTS

ILLUSTRATIONS

The numbers given in brackets below refer to *Käthe Kollwitz; Verzeichnis des graphischen Werkes* by Dr. August Klipstein. This is the definitive guide or catalogue raisonné to the known graphic works of Käthe Kollwitz. All of her etchings, lithographs, and woodcuts are reproduced in it, with complete information on each one given in German. Eight hundred copies of this essential reference were published in 1955. Copies may be found in the art collections of major libraries.

FOREWORD

This book presents the art of Käthe Kollwitz in the light of her remarkable life and personality. It is thus both an "art book" and a biography. As much as possible, primary attention has been focused on her art. Nevertheless the book devotes far more text to the actions, events, and intentions of this great artist's long, rich life than does any other work thus far published, insofar as the authors know. Even so, much has had to be omitted for reasons of length.

This volume is written mainly for nonspecialists in art. Accordingly it avoids most of the formalities and scholarly apparatus of art-historical monographs. No assumption has been made that readers necessarily will have prior familiarity with the art of Käthe Kollwitz. The authors hope, in fact, that many thousands, meeting that art for the first time through this book, will be moved to make it a continuing part of their lives.

Opinions and interpretations contained in the following pages are those of the authors, unless otherwise indicated.

ACKNOWLEDGMENTS

Many persons, far and near, have aided the authors with information, comment, encouragement, and other courtesies of various kinds, including valuable assistance in locating and securing reproductions of the works here included. To all of them our thanks are offered; and especially to:

Dr. Hans Kollwitz, son of the artist, of Berlin (West), and Maria Matray, niece of the artist, of Munich, Germany.

Drs. Heinz Lüdecke and Werner Timm, art historians and critics, of Berlin (East); Rolf Recknagel, Fachschule für Bibliothekare, Leipzig.

Dr. and Frau Hans Ebert, Kupferstichkabinett, Staatliche Museen zu Berlin; Herr Harri Nündel and Frau Gisela Josten, Deutsche Akademie der Künste, Berlin; Drs. Susanne Heiland & Karl-Heinz Mehnert of the Museum der Bildenden Künste, Leipzig (all of the German Democratic Republic).

Also: Drs. Matthias Winner and Barbara Mundt, Staatliche Museen (Preussische Kulturbesitz); and Miss Elisabeth Killy, Akademie der Künste, all of Berlin (West).

Also: Hans-Heinrich Richter, Director of the Deutsche Fotothek Dresden; the Kunsthalle of Bremen; the Verkehrsamt of Cologne; Dr. Gisela Bergsträsser, Hessische Landesmuseum, Darmstadt; Dr. Dieter Graf, Kunstmuseum, Düsseldorf; S. Mahn, Staatliche Galerie, Halle; Dr. Michael Schwartz, Kunsthalle, Hamburg; Dr. Isa Lohmann-Siems, Ernst Barlach Haus, Hamburg; Dr. Gisela Fiedler, Kaiser Wilhelm Museum, Krefeld; Herr Otto Feld, Kunstgeschichtliches Institut, Gutenberg Universität, Mainz; and Dr. Gunther Thiem, Graphische Sammlung, Staatsgalerie, Stuttgart.

Also: Dr. Walter Koschatzky, Director, Graphische Sammlung Albertina, Vienna; M. Jean Adhémar, Conservateur en Chef, Cabinet des Estampes, Bibliothèque Nationale, Paris; and Mrs. Elisheva Cohen, Acting Chief Curator, The Israel Museum, Jerusalem. Likewise: the Directors, Marlborough Fine Art (London) Ltd. and Miss Brigitte Drakes of their photographic department; Edward Telesford, Photographic Service of the British Museum; and, in a very special way, to Mrs. Ruth Forster, London, England.

On this side of the Atlantic, and along the Pacific Coast—we express our thanks to Dorothy Brown of Malibu, Professor Emeritus of Art, UCLA; Donald L. Dame, Director of Galleries, California State College at Long Beach; Ross De Vean, Beverly Hills; Ebria Feinblatt, Curator, Prints and Drawings, Los Angeles County Museum of Art; Dr. and Mrs. Marvin S. Freilich, Beverly Hills; Drs. Frederic Kohner and Meyer Krakowski, Los Angeles; Ernst Matray; Mrs. Charlotte Monasch; Henry Seldis, art critic, Los Angeles *Times;* Kate Steinitz, distinguished scholar and art lover; and last—only because of the accidents of alphabetical order—Josephine and Jake Zeitlin, Los Angeles.

Also, outside the immediate area of greater Los Angeles, to: Herbert W. Andree, Acting Registrar, Santa Barbara Museum of Art; Dr. E. Gunther Trochee, Director, and Fenton Kastner, Curator, Achenbach Foundation for Graphic Arts, San Francisco.

Likewise, on the East Coast of the United States, to: Karl Kup, Curator of Prints, New York Public Library; Mrs. Nada Saporiti, Librarian, Metropolitan Museum of Art; Dr. Otto Kallir, Galerie St. Etienne—all of New York City.

Also: Katharine Shepard, Assistant Curator, Graphic Arts, National Gallery, Washington, D.C.; Mrs. Roger Fisher, Office of Associate Director, Fogg Art Museum, Harvard University, Cambridge; and Henry Ernest, Montreal, Canada.

We are grateful for the use of many sources of material in the UCLA Art Library under Mrs. Jean Moore, Art Librarian; and for reference works in the Graduate Research Library of UCLA, for use of which we thank University Librarian Robert Vosper and his cooperative staff.

KÄTHE KOLLWITZ
Life in Art

chapter 1
to 1884

Family and Girlhood

"I agree that my art has purpose. *I want to be effective* in this time when people are so helpless and in need of aid." So Käthe Kollwitz wrote as she reflected on the work which was the voice, the weapon, and the glory of her life.

That long, memorable life ended more than a quarter of a century ago, but her works continue to express her opposition to war, brutality, hunger, exploitation, and discrimination, and her dedication to human dignity and brotherhood.

This book, devoted to her art and her life, seeks to show the one as the expression of the other and both as products of her dynamic, troubled period. Despite the years that have gone by, it is basically our own period also.

The life of Käthe Kollwitz began in Königsberg, then the capital of the German province of East Prussia. As an artist she became one of the most effective proponents of peace. Yet she was a native of a part of the world whose history has made it a kind of symbol of incessant warmaking and conquests.

The territory that became East Prussia had been populated originally by Slavic peoples. Then in the thirteenth century it had been conquered by the warlike and ruthless order of Teutonic Knights. In what had been a small Slavic settlement near the mouth of the Tegel River these Teutonic Knights established their principal city, naming it Königsberg, meaning the "Mountain (or Citadel) of the King." There, by tradition, was crowned each new monarch of the Hohenzollern dynasty—the ambitious, aggressive, and endlessly conspiratorial kings of Prussia.

One may look in vain for the name Königsberg on the latest maps. Events since 1945 reversed the bloody history of the previous seven centuries. The site is now called Kaliningrad, and it is the principal city of a region taken over by the Soviet Union after the defeat of Germany at the close of World War II, in the spring of 1945.

On July 8, 1867, a new daughter was born to Katharina and Karl Schmidt of Königsberg. They named her Käthe Ida. Käthe (pronounced KAY-teh) was a name derived from her mother's, Katharina.

The Schmidts were no aristocrats. Karl Schmidt, in fact, was a mason— a master mason who had become a building contractor. Nevertheless the Schmidts were distinguished people. They were extraordinarily admirable as individuals and even more so as a family group because of their unusual intelligence, firm moral fiber, self-respect, courage, and strength of conviction.

All this was the more noteworthy against the background of general conformity, abject acceptance of authority, and even of servility that typified the most prominent citizens of Königsberg and of all Prussia at the time. A proper evaluation of the Schmidts must begin a generation earlier, with Julius Rupp, father of Katharina and grandfather of the infant Käthe. Rupp had been, in succession, a teacher, university professor, clergyman, lay preacher, and a political leader and legislator.

Once Julius Rupp had held an eminently respectable and respected post as chaplain to the military garrison of Königsberg, that is, to the armed forces of the Hohenzollern rulers. But he had given up this secure post when he could no longer reconcile its implications with his conscience and beliefs. Courageously he had set himself outside the established and official Protestant Church of East Prussia and had founded a dissident group—Germany's first Free Religious Congregation. In its beliefs and practices this group could be compared to the Unitarians in the United States today. However, to the conservative and ultrapietistic religious establishment of East Prussia in the mid-nineteenth century, the members of the new movement around Julius Rupp seemed scarcely better than atheists—outrageously deviant in their attitudes and a festering thorn in the flesh of officialdom.

The Free Religious Congregation did not call Grandfather Rupp their priest, minister, or even pastor. They used no such titles. Instead he was merely known as their "speaker"—meaning spiritual leader. He neither claimed nor accepted for himself any spiritual authority beyond that of the other members of his congregation.

The Protestant churches of Prussia at this time were dominated by docile supporters of the Prussian kaiser, Friedrich Wilhelm IV. Julius Rupp and his group were active opponents of this state-supported church. They paid dearly, but willingly, for their opposition. In the year 1849 alone, the Prussian police broke up more than one hundred of their meetings.

Not only in religion but also in other areas of life powerful ferments were at work in this period. A great economic depression in 1847 had led to a series of attempted revolts in 1848. There were uprisings in Italy and Switzerland. In France, King Louis Philippe (1773–1850) of Bourbon was ousted and a republic proclaimed. In Vienna, the champion of European reaction, Count Metternich (1773–1859), was forced to flee to England. Karl Marx (1818–1883) and Friedrich Engels (1820–1895), having escaped from Germany to France, issued their historic *Communist Manifesto*, concluding with the summons: "Workers of the world, unite! You have nothing to lose but your chains. You have a world to gain!"

At that time Germany, as such, did not exist. Instead there were many separate German kingdoms and principalities of which Prussia was the most powerful. But even tightly ruled Prussia, with all its military apparatus, did not escape the mounting social discontent. On March 18, 1848, protesting workers gathered before the palace of the kaiser in Berlin and were attacked by his troops. More than 180 of the demonstrators were killed before the rest forced some 14,000 troops and many guns to be withdrawn from the city. The crown prince, who had been in command of the troops, fled in disguise to England where he stayed for some time.

However, the 1848 revolutionary movement in Prussia was eventually crushed, and years of repression and reaction followed. Great numbers of progressive and free-spirited Germans fled their native land—about one million and a half in all. Most of them went to the United States. They included many of their country's moral and intellectual leaders.

Often Käthe and her brother and sisters heard Grandfather Julius Rupp refer in public or family gatherings to "the March dead"—meaning those who fell in Berlin that March day of 1848. He and Käthe's parents identified themselves with these remembered martyrs and their cause. And so did Käthe, with unwavering sympathy and growing understanding. In 1913, when she was a woman of forty-six, she was to create a series of three lithographs called *March Cemetery*, showing German workers reverently and silently looking down on the flower-strewn graves of their martyrs of sixty-five years before.

Julius Rupp fought for his progressive convictions within the established framework of government as well as in the Free Religious Congregation. In 1849 he was chosen a member of the Prussian legislative body, the House of Deputies. During the subsequent reactionary era of 1850–1854 he was imprisoned many times. A ban was issued to halt lectures he was to give at the University of Königsberg, where the great German philosopher Immanuel Kant (1724–1804) had taught some decades earlier. The reason given was typical: ". . . for . . . general welfare of the state." Prosecution and persecution did not weaken Rupp's resolve. He survived without compromise, and in 1862, only a few years before Käthe's birth, was once again elected a deputy.

This courageous man was very much a part of the family world in which young Käthe grew up, for he lived on, active and influential, until she was seventeen years old. Rupp was a man of benevolence and good will as well as courage. His character was infused with the communal ideals typical of early Christianity. On his gravestone were carved words expressive of his concept of life: "Man is not here to be happy, but to fulfill his duty."

Käthe felt for her grandfather a shy respect and even veneration, but no close personal warmth. To her he seemed to stand above everyday things, quite different from his wife, Käthe's grandmother, who was immersed in everyday affairs.

When Käthe, her sisters, and brother went with their parents to the Sunday meetings of the Free Congregation in Königsberg, it was Grandfather Rupp who led the service, speaking with eloquent conviction. He was also the children's religious teacher. Later her father took over religious education for the Free Congregation, and Käthe felt relieved, for he was less rigid than Grandfather Rupp. Ethics, as her father taught it, seemed easier for her to understand.

While Käthe was growing up, the members of the Free Congregation were no longer being jailed for their views and efforts to organize, but their memories of past persecutions remained strong. Käthe acquired early a deep sense of the needs and misfortunes of others. She owed this not only to the influence of Grandfather Rupp but also to her own father, for Karl Schmidt was a man no less outstanding and independent.

Schmidt, born in 1825 to a poor family, had been able to gain an education only through the generosity of a stranger. He had studied law and could have become a successful and wealthy lawyer. But even before he could begin to practice he realized that this career was not for him. His religious views and socialist sympathies would not permit him, in good conscience, to serve as part of the legal machinery of the kaiser's Prussia, a militaristic state.

Instead Schmidt learned the trade of a mason. First he served an apprenticeship, then went on to become a master builder. Later he married Katharina, eldest of Julius Rupp's six children. She was twelve years younger than Schmidt.

When Rupp retired as spiritual leader of the Free Congregation Schmidt replaced him, giving up his building trade to do so. Thus from early manhood Schmidt had been a convinced follower of ideals that many years later Käthe found in the Communist circles of Germany during the early 1920s.

Käthe's mother, Katharina, resembled her father, Julius Rupp, in mind and temperament. She became an understanding though undemonstrative mother, quietly attuned to the emotional and mental needs of her family. Indeed this was later true also of Käthe as mother and wife.

Katharina Schmidt was a cultured woman. She was widely read in German and also in English, being especially fond of Shakespeare, Shelley, and Byron. Like her husband she was talented in drawing and in her spare time sometimes made copies of paintings by old masters.

Until Käthe was nine the Schmidt family lived near the banks of Königsberg's Pregel River. Then her father's increasing success as a builder enabled them to move to a better house. But always, in her vivid memories, the riverside house remained her favorite. Near it stood a shed in which plaster casts were made. Fascinated, Käthe often watched the workmen form these figures. The odor of moist plaster lingered on in her memory and the love of sculpture never left her.

Such stimulation came to her from many directions. In fact Käthe, reflecting on her own girlhood in afteryears, concluded that during the receptive and sensitive early stages of life, every child can be regarded as gifted, and that nourishment to develop these gifts can come to the child from any direction. It was her good fortune to have parents and a family who provided abundant sustenance for her own great gifts.

Yet her development was not easy or free from conflicts. The Schmidts worried about their young Käthe, and with cause. Her skin was sallow; she seemed nervous and slept poorly. Nightmares tormented her. She had sudden seizures of screaming, crying, struggling, day and night. Her parents feared for a time that she might be epileptic. However they remained patient, never using blows or force to restrain her.

Later the crying spells gave way to moods of melancholy that endured for hours, even days. The nightmares ceased to plague her by the time she was past twenty. The depressions, however, continued taking hold of her at intervals throughout her life, darkening her moods and often her works. Though she loved laughter and fun, she was stamped with an underlying seriousness that nothing could dissolve for long.

Käthe matured, however, in this atmosphere of warmth and affection. The love of literature, art, and learning was a part of the Schmidt household. More important, the parents respected their children's individual rights to grow, to find, and to fulfill themselves. For their time they were a most permissive family but by no means an indifferent or distant one.

The oldest of the surviving Schmidt children was Konrad. Next came Julie, then Käthe, then Lise, the youngest. Two other children, born earlier than Konrad, had died, and Benjamin, born after Lise, died of meningitis when just a year old.

Memories of Benjamin's illness and death were deeply stamped on Käthe's mind. As a mature woman and even in her old age she recalled how she had ached with love and pity as her reserved mother had grieved silently for Benjamin. More than one great work of Käthe's was to embody such desperate, helpless grief. Others reversed the roles: with the living child clinging to the mother threatened by death.

Käthe was tormented by feelings of guilt because of a strange circumstance that had occurred at the time of Benjamin's death. Her father had wanted his children to have worthwhile playthings and had given them large building blocks—not unlike some of the better educational toys of today. From these Käthe had built for her own use a temple to Venus, based on pictures she had seen in some of the many books in the Schmidt household. She was playing at worship in this temple when her mother and father, quietly coming into the room, had told her that Benjamin had died. Käthe was terror-stricken. God, she thought, was punishing them all for her sacrifices to the pagan diety Venus.

Käthe could feel no love for this stern, punishing God of the Christians, though she did feel an affection for Jesus, whose gentle humanity was stressed by the Free Religious Congregation in Königsberg.

As a girl and throughout a long life afterward, Käthe was closest to her younger sister Lisbeth, called Lise. They were inseparable and even came to look alike when they grew old. As children they played together endlessly, cutting out and coloring paper dolls that had been made to represent the

Pensive, thoughtful Käthe Schmidt was in her mid-teens when she and twenty-two other members of her family posed for this undated photograph. Previously unpublished, this picture shows Käthe (13) standing near her father, Karl Schmidt (12) and her mother, Katharina Rupp Schmidt (9).

Left of Käthe stand her brother, Konrad (11), and her older sister, Julie (10). Seated left of her mother is Käthe's younger sister, Lisbeth, called Lise (8). Farthest left stands her mother's sister, Käthe's Aunt Benina Prengel (3), behind her husband, Uncle Max Prengel (2), and their four children (1, 4, 5, 6). Just left of Käthe's mother stands her unmarried sister, Aunt Lina Rupp (7). The bearded man right of Käthe is her mother's brother, Uncle Julius Rupp (14). Below him sits his wife, Aunt Lina Rupp (17), holding their two children (15, 16).

At right, the seated man with beard is Uncle Karl Rentel (19), and behind him his wife, Aunt Toni Rentel (18), sister of Käthe's mother. Farthest right stands her mother's brother, Uncle Theobald Rupp (21). Below him sits his wife, Aunt Gertrude Rupp, and their two children (20, 23). *Courtesy of a member of the family of Käthe Kollwitz.*

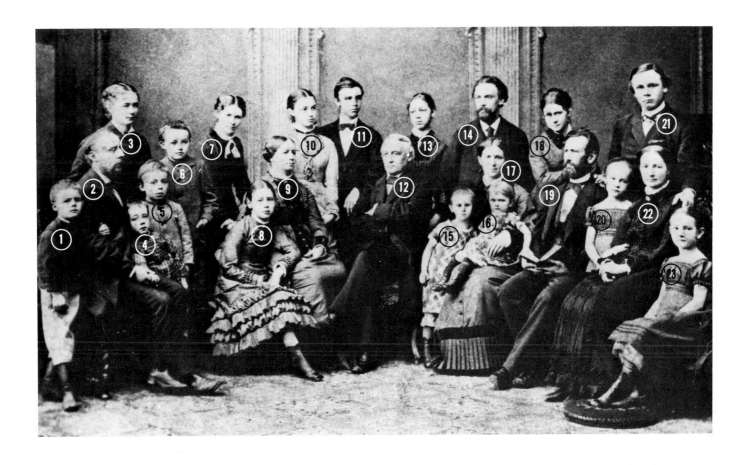

characters in famous dramas. In the summertime they staged outdoor per-formances of these plays, Käthe taking the lead in organizing the family dramatics. Their parents watched appreciatively from a distance, continuing to give them the great gift of noninterference.

Dramatization was deeply rooted in the temperaments and lives of the younger Schmidt sisters. Käthe herself, though an untheatrical and even reserved personality, always had a strongly dramatic imagination and out-look. Her mature art focused frequently on dramatic, or even melodra-matic, situations and confrontations involving common people. One of her most important early successes in art was inspired by Hauptmann's historical drama *The Weavers*.

Her formal schooling, like the rest of her life as a girl, was marked by relative freedom from the hidebound patterns prevalent elsewhere in Ger-many. Her parents and grandparents regarded the existing public schools as rigid and reactionary, serving mainly to mold children into docile servitors of the Prussian state. Hence the Schmidt children and many of their cousins were taught in small private groups.

Käthe herself did not especially enjoy this family-made schooling. True,

7

she loved literature and history, but she was poor in mathematics. Her father, in summer, served as arithmetic coach.

He had noted, however, Käthe's talents along a different line. Her extraordinary scribblings and doodlings on bits of paper that had been left over from his building plans revealed beyond doubt that she had an exceptional talent for drawing.

The school that Käthe most relished was supplied for her by the world of Königsberg's manual workers. For hours on end she and Lise were allowed to wander around the worker-filled streets, docks, and warehouses. She watched with admiration the strength, skill, and endurance of the workers. Sometimes the girls visited the railway station and stared at the foreign passengers pausing en route from the Russian capital, St. Petersburg, to the French capital, Paris. Käthe was grateful that her parents never forbade their wanderings or questioned where they had been. The Schmidts' young friends envied these freedoms.

Usually Käthe was rather silent with young people her own age, but there were many gay parties at the Schmidt home when she danced exuberantly and endlessly. The Schmidts always managed, too, to find money for books and theater. Their home was filled with books to which the children had full, free access. There were no banned shelves or taboos. Käthe, ever responsive to poetry and drama, steeped herself in the German classics: a fine, big edition of Schiller (1759–1805) with engravings by Kaulbach and, above all, in the works of Goethe (1749–1832). He became the constant companion of her thoughts for a lifetime. His books were to be the last read to her, and her old hands felt for his mask above her bed just before her death in 1945.

By general acclaim Johann Wolfgang von Goethe was the greatest man of letters to have used the German language. That opinion was held unswervingly by Käthe Schmidt Kollwitz and it remains today the judgment of most critics and literary historians. Goethe was a many-sided creator: a superb lyric poet, a rich and often subtle novelist and writer of novellas, a playwright and dramatic director, a critic, and even—at least in his own view—a natural scientist. Today he could be described as a great amateur of science, whose principal theories have historical interest rather than present value. He probably would have resented such a description, however.

The literary world of Goethe was vast and ever-enthralling for Käthe. Yet it must be noted that in her own art she did not later on reflect Goethe's attitudes. He himself was basically conservative, allied in his life with the aristocracy of the small court of Weimar, whose duke he served as minister, writer-in-residence, and—so to speak—cultural ornament. As he grew older Goethe became more lofty and Olympian in his views. Some might even say that he became increasingly snobbish, reactionary, and stuffy.

If the mature Goethe could have conversed face to face with the girl Käthe Schmidt or the woman Käthe Kollwitz, they would assuredly have differed definitely, perhaps sharply, in their basic social and political attitudes. In his later years Goethe went so far as to suggest that it was better to tolerate injustice than to permit disorder. Käthe was dedicated to the contrary conviction: nothing—neither tradition nor propriety nor fear of change—could excuse injustice. Social injustice was for her the greatest of all disorders. She saw its harmful effects around her reflected in the faces and figures of the poor, the hungry, the disappointed, and the degraded.

Despite the enormous enthusiasm which led her to memorize large segments of Goethe's poetry, Käthe could never share his lofty unconcern for the lot of the common people. For her Goethe was a "lord of language," in the phrase used by Oscar Wilde (1854–1900). But her clear vision and strong mind enabled her to form and act on opinions that Goethe seldom would have tolerated.

Käthe's brother, Konrad, the eldest Schmidt child, helped launch her on the reading of the great and, by the standards of the time, even dangerous moderns: Ibsen (1829–1906), Zola (1840–1902), Tolstoy (1828–1910), Dostoevsky (1821–1881), Gorki (1868–1936), and others. She even read Karl Kautsky's (1854–1938) interpretation of the ideas of Karl Marx. But it was art that won her ever-increasing attention, and she studied with especial fascination the engravings of Hogarth, and then the great graphic works of Rembrandt and Goya.

Käthe began to have crushes early. As a child and as an adolescent she was constantly in love with other people, both male and female. Her first "affair" was with a boy upstairs. They traded secret kisses, which they called their "refreshment." He, however, doubted he could marry a girl from a Free Congregation family, and she feared that she could never bear so frightful a last name as the one he happened to have. Their dilemma was solved when he and his family moved away. Käthe was left shattered.

From then on she fell in love repeatedly, sometimes with women. Seldom did she reveal her feelings to the person involved. Her mother and she were too reserved to talk together about such things, and her growing inner control kept these crushes hidden.

Later, analyzing the roles of love and art in her life, she wrote that even though for her attraction for the masculine sex dominated, she had found an inclination toward her own sex which she grew to understand only in her maturity. She came then to believe that such bisexuality is essential for the highest attainments in art. The masculine element within her, she felt, strengthened her own creative work.

Many confusions resulted from Käthe's eager reading, constant curiosity, and almost total lack of information. From a misunderstood work of fiction she got the notion that she, or any girl, could have a child with no physical cause. She received some small help from Konrad, who understood, from his own needs, some of hers. Typically their communication was without words. Konrad got the message from a drawing by Käthe that he had found. Thereafter he tried to steer her away from reading that would be likely to add to her confusions.

As she matured her unmistakable artistic abilities developed also. "A pity that Katuschen is not a boy," her father once remarked, using his favorite pet name for her in a comment that clearly reflected the world's attitude toward women in the arts.

However, before she had reached her fourteenth birthday he showed his deeper understanding and vision by arranging special drawing lessons for her. She sensed that her father, noting that she was not pretty, expected that love affairs would not arise to distract her from art.

Rudolph Mauer, a copper engraver of Königsberg, became her first instructor in the summer of 1891. She was one of several girls in his class, drawing heads from plaster casts in the traditional manner. From the Königsberg street below came the sounds of the hot city, impressing themselves indelibly on the mind of the young girl.

She was eager and earnest and made good progress, pleasing her parents with every new drawing. Much later Mauer, at her request, gave her an introduction to the mysteries of etching and intaglio printing from the finished etched plates.

Other members of the Schmidt family were also creative. Konrad composed dramatic tragedies, which were then performed by the family, including Käthe. (Later her own son Hans was to do the same in Berlin.)

Their father read aloud to them, especially the powerful revolutionary poems of Ferdinand Freiligrath (1810–1876). His *From the Dead to the Living* was a summons to continue the revolt begun by the martyrs of March 1848. In her rich fantasy world, Käthe saw herself on the barricades, loading rifles for her father and Konrad.

Freiligrath, like Heinrich Heine (1797–1856) and some other German writers, portrayed the miseries and protest of the weavers in Silesia, whose 1844 uprising had served as a prelude to 1848. Käthe was later to make an unforgettable series of prints on this subject.

She was shaken when her father read aloud the poet's German translation of Thomas Hood's *The Song of the Shirt*, describing the misery of workers in England in 1843:

> *With fingers weary and worn,*
> *With eyelids heavy and red,*
> *A woman sat, in unwomanly rags,*
> *Plying her needle and thread—*
> *   Stitch! stitch, stitch!*
> *In poverty, hunger, and dirt,*
> *And still with a voice of dolorous pitch*
> *She sang the "Song of the Shirt!"*

A later verse from that poem strangely suggests themes later chosen by Käthe Kollwitz, the artist:

> *But why do I talk of Death?*
> *That Phantom of grisly bone,*
> *I hardly fear his terrible shape,*
> *It seems so like my own—*
> *It seems so like my own,*
> *Because of the fasts I keep,*
> *Oh! God! that bread should be so dear,*
> *And flesh and blood so cheap!*

Käthe was only sixteen when she made one of her first drawings clearly showing members of the working class. It was inspired by another of Freiligrath's poems. Throughout her life works of literature continued to move her to powerful portrayals in line and tone.

Stimulated by sights at the docks and work places of Königsberg, she continued drawing. Her parents sometimes asked her why she did not select what they called "beautiful" subjects. But these subjects *were* beautiful, she would reply. Her sister Lise years later offered a possible explanation: pretty faces did not show the longing, the striving toward an unattainable goal that attracted Käthe; but so-called ugly people did.

Even as a girl in her teens Käthe had formed one opinion she would never give up: beauty, or attractiveness, was found in human intensity, in the physical reflection of the labors, the efforts, the cares and concerns, the loves, losses, and griefs that made up the lives of real and ordinary people.

The godlike but imaginary forms created by Greek and Roman sculptors, or even those shaped by the Renaissance artists who had drawn on the classical ideals of flawless perfection—these held for Käthe Schmidt neither charm nor interest. They lacked, for her, the intensity, the vitality, the reality which alone seemed important for her own approach to art.

Perhaps by this time she had not expressed it to herself so simply or clearly, but she might almost have used the words which were to be uttered later by the French painter Paul Gauguin (1848–1903): "Ugliness can be beautiful; prettiness never."

chapter 2
1884-1891

First Steps in Art

Käthe turned seventeen in July of 1884. The events of that year were in many ways decisive for the rest of her life. In that year her grandfather, Julius Rupp, died at the age of seventy-five. Käthe, with her mother and sister Lise made her first and unforgettable journey to the great German cities of Berlin and Munich. Also in 1884 her parents decided that Käthe as a full-time and independent student of art should be given the chance to show how far she could go with her obvious talents.

Finally before the end of 1884 she became engaged to Karl Kollwitz, the gentle young man who became her husband, her devoted friend, and lifelong companion.

By 1884 Käthe's older sister, Julie, had married and was living in Berlin, the swiftly growing capital of the German Reich that had come into being little more than a dozen years before. With Käthe and Lise, Frau Katharina Schmidt went to visit her daughter Julie.

Through Julie they met one of her neighbors, a young writer, then almost unknown, named Gerhart Hauptmann (1862–1946). One evening Hauptmann entertained them in his own home. It was, for Käthe, a never-to-be-forgotten event. She, like the other women of the company, wore roses in her hair and drank wine while listening to Hauptmann read from Shakespeare's *Julius Caesar* in the superb German translation by August Schlegel and Ludwig Tieck.

Hauptmann's later career, long and often distinguished, though marred by many discreditable political changes and compromises, was to contrast sharply with the later life of the young Fräulein Käthe Schmidt, who sat rose-bedecked, entranced by Hauptmann's declamation and his wine.

After Berlin, Frau Schmidt and her excited daughters traveled on to Munich, capital of Bavaria and at that time the principal art center of the new Reich. It was, in fact, considered to be second only to Paris in the vitality of its art activities. Käthe was carried away by the masterpieces of great painters and graphic artists of the past displayed in Munich's famous Pinakothek picture gallery.

She was especially enthralled by the works of Rubens (1577–1640), with all their sweep and tonal resonance. She carried with her—as she did so often during her life—a volume of Goethe's poetry. In its margins she wrote rhapsodic approvals of Rubens alongside her praises of Goethe.

From Munich Frau Schmidt and her daughters traveled to Switzerland, where they lingered for a time in the resort of Engadin for the sake of Katharina's health.

While there they were joined by Käthe's brother, Konrad, fresh from London. Karl Marx, the great founder of scientific socialism and author of *Das Kapital*, had died during 1883 in England at the age of sixty-five. However, his close friend and coworker, Friedrich Engels, now sixty-four, was still very much alive and productive there. While in England Konrad had visited much with Engels and other socialists close to him.

By this time Konrad had become a full-fledged scientific socialist, regarded by many as a coming young man in the growing socialist movement, which advocated that the workers own and control the means of production. Käthe was deeply influenced by the views of her elder brother.

Konrad became for her a kind of political guide and mentor. His friends and hers increasingly came from the same circles in Königsberg. They were, in general, the most alert, informed, progressive, and humanitarian-minded of the youth in that provincial capital.

Among them were an orphaned brother and sister named Kollwitz, who came from a poor family. Karl Kollwitz was a close friend of Konrad, while Karl's sister was a friend of Käthe and Lise Schmidt. Karl and Käthe had known each other well for years. Now twenty-one, Karl had become a student of medicine. He, like Konrad, was a socialist—or a Social Democrat, as it was called in Germany. Karl was also an ardent admirer of the pensive, intelligent, intense Käthe, and she was drawn to this gentle, sincere young man.

She was only seventeen when they sealed their affections with an engagement. Marriage, of course, would have to wait until Karl could complete his medical training and earn a living as a practicing physician. Meantime, Käthe would use the period of waiting—inactivity was not in her nature.

By this time Konrad had already left Königsberg to live as a student in Berlin where he studied economics and literature at the great university there. Käthe, too, wanted to benefit by what Berlin had to offer, and now her parents decided that her hope and ambition should be given opportunity. They agreed, as a trial, to give her a year there as an art student, living in a respectable boardinghouse or *pension*, and studying at the School for Women Artists.

Sex-segregated education in art was standard at that time. Not until early in the twentieth century were women admitted to the same art classes as men. After all, the study of art included the anatomy of the nude human body.

In Berlin, Käthe's principal teacher was the remarkable, vigorous, courageous, and youthful Karl Stauffer-Bern (1857–1891). Swiss-born, aged only twenty-seven, he was a painter, an etcher, a sculptor, and even a poet. He was widely known in Berlin's small but swiftly growing art circles. Stauffer-Bern himself had no high opinion of most of the art being produced in Berlin. He looked on it as imitative, derivative, and timidly traditional.

In the new student from East Prussia, Fräulein Schmidt, he soon recognized talent; she in turn found in him a superior teacher. The rest of her life she remained grateful for the good fortune that had brought her early to an instructor of excellence, understanding, and free spirit.

Had the customary teaching plan been followed, Käthe would have concentrated first on painting heads of live models under Stauffer-Bern's supervision. However, at her father's suggestion, Käthe showed this new teacher one of her Königsberg drawings, inspired by Freiligrath's poem *Emigrating*. Stauffer-Bern recognized in this work something strong and distinctive. In fact, it reminded him in some ways of work by his friend, the accomplished artist and sculptor Max Klinger (1857–1920). Fräulein Schmidt, with Stauffer-Bern's advice and encouragement, turned more and more to developing her drawing instead of painting.

She had not heard of Klinger previously, but now she sought out his work. His series of etchings called *A Life* happened to be currently on exhibition in Berlin. They were badly hung in a small, remote room, but when she stood before them, Käthe Schmidt felt as if great gates were swinging open before her. Here was an artist who already had moved confidently in directions she had felt dimly but intensely that she wanted to follow in her own work.

Later, in Munich, she found and studied still other etchings by Klinger. By that time he had become so popular among art students that she had to wait her turn in the print room to leaf through the Klinger portfolios.

In the years that followed Klinger remained a deep and lasting influence on her work. It was typical of her reserve and respect for the privacy of others that she met the artist himself face to face only two or three times. She freely acknowledged to the world her great sense of indebtedness to him, even after she had largely purged from her own works the symbolism and allegory that were so prominent in Klinger's.

Some forty-five years after she first encountered his work in Berlin she wrote that his art had made the strongest impression of any she received in her youth. And after Klinger died in 1920 Käthe Kollwitz spoke at his grave as representative of the Free Secession artist group of Berlin. In a noteworthy eulogy she publicly affirmed his influence on her own work and expressed her gratitude. A decade later she noted with regret that Klinger was no longer admired by young artists.

In the mid-1880s Klinger was essentially an exponent of the new Naturalistic style then in vogue in Germany. It was a style opposed, sometimes quite deliberately, to another and increasingly influential art style called Impressionism, which emanated largely from Paris. Klinger's Naturalism combined great precision of detail with almost breathtaking virtuosity in the techniques of drawing and etching. For the taste of the 1970s Klinger often seems far too literal and limited to be important, save perhaps as an illustrator. However his range and productivity still astound.

The "isms" of art history and criticism are often confusing and sometimes completely contradictory. In her own work Käthe Kollwitz shunned fads, schools, and formal styles. Even her early and enduring esteem for Klinger did not influence her to follow Naturalism in her own graphic works and drawings.

In Paris during 1874—just a few years after the defeat France suffered in the Franco-Prussian War—thirty independent artists who felt themselves divorced from the hidebound traditions of the academic style held a joint exhibition. One of them, Claude Monet (1840–1926), included a painting which he had entitled "Impression, Sunrise" because it was in fact just that, his impression—not a reproduction—of the light and color of a rising sun.

LEFT:
The artist at about twenty years of age, when she was still Käthe Schmidt, gifted art student from Königsberg, East Prussia.

RIGHT:
Self-portrait made with pen, sepia, and India ink, when the artist was about twenty-two years old. It is signed with her maiden name, Schmidt, and dated 1889.
Deutsche Fotothek Dresden.

16

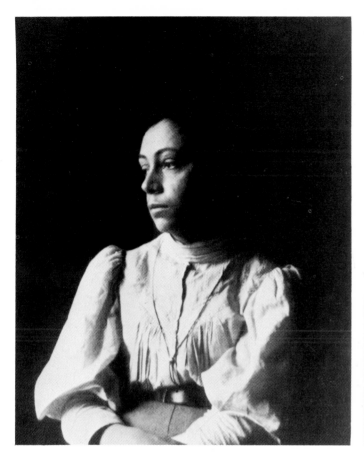
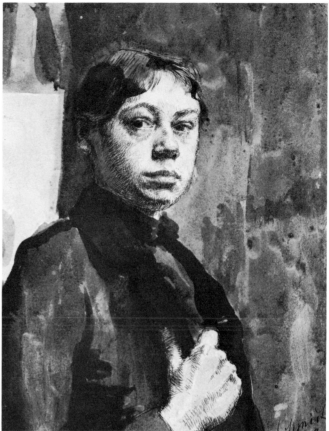

A critic, Alfred Leroy, writing of the exhibition, seized upon the word and applied it as a disparaging name to the entire group. To him they were mere impressionists. The artists involved raged and protested, but the name stuck. These unorthodox exiles from the established salon were henceforth to be known as Impressionists.

The name Naturalism, on the other hand, had originally been used to label the work of novelists, short-story writers, or dramatists who sought to portray ordinary, even ugly, aspects of life in a completely and exhaustively realistic way. Naturalism was then stretched or extended to comparable tendencies in painting and graphic arts.

Käthe Schmidt, an enthusiastic young art student in Berlin, worried little about schools, styles, or manifestos of art movements. She had work that challenged and absorbed her, and she was beginning to make friends with other art students. Her closest friendship was formed with a slender girl named Emma Jeep. They sat together in an evening class that was supposed to reveal the mysteries of human anatomy. Their instructor brought to class a chest filled with loose human bones, which were then passed from hand to hand among his young female art students. They learned the shapes of the bones but remained unclear as to how they were fitted together in the human body.

Emma Jeep made a mild sensation and won the tribute of silent laughter from Fräulein Schmidt by asking the instructor, "What about that missing rib bone?" clearly referring to the rib taken from Adam to make Eve, as told in the Bible. The instructor answered promptly and coolly, "Oh, the missing rib grew back again," thus winning the admiration of his students for his presence of mind.

Emma Jeep at first thought this dark-haired, dark-eyed Käthe Schmidt looked interesting but strange, and told her so. Far from cooling, their acquaintance thereafter deepened into a close and enduring friendship. Soon they were calling each other simply Jeep and Schmidt. They continued to do so for the next sixty years.

Jeep, who seems from the beginning to have recognized the great artistic gifts of Schmidt, did not finally become a practicing artist herself, save for occasional sketches. She later married a writer, Arthur Bonus, who died in 1940.

Following a year of productive study and work in Berlin, Käthe returned home to Königsberg. Stauffer-Bern had urged Karl Schmidt to send his daughter back for a second year of art study in Berlin. However, the decision was made that Käthe should continue instead in Königsberg. The official art academy there did not admit women, so she and another young woman had instruction in painting from an artist named Emil Neide (1843–1908). His own paintings had attracted attention because they included many criminal and underworld subjects. Undoubtedly this resulted in part from the fact that his brother was a police commissioner.

One of Neide's most sensational pictures, entitled "Weary of Life," dealt with a suicide. It provoked comment as far away as America. Though only eighteen, Käthe Schmidt was critical of Neide's work. Some of his crime paintings she regarded as weak, even trashy. However, she approved of one small painting of his, "The Scene of the Crime." It was a sober portrayal of the investigation of a murder in a gravel pit. Some of her own later choices of subjects show a certain similarity, for they deal with grim, even painful, situations but are free from sensationalism or sentimentality.

During this period in Königsberg, Käthe drew harbor and dock workers and poor people at work and at rest. She also did some portraits of friends and relatives. Her father wanted her to paint a genre picture, portraying an everyday event in a manner that tells a story. Somewhat unwillingly Käthe did turn out "Before the Ball," but even while she worked on it the subject remained uninteresting to her.

Her father, however, was pleased. Next year, when Käthe was studying in Munich, he had it framed and, unknown to her, submitted it to an East Prussian traveling art exhibit. It found a purchaser, who even went on to order a sequel to be called "After the Ball." However, because of a slight mixup in the mails this order reached another Fräulein Schmidt, not Käthe, who was delighted it had missed her. By this time neither she nor her fellow art students in Munich approved such sentimental themes.

To Käthe it seemed that she had made small gain during her Königsberg work in 1887. Neide's painting instruction had benefited her very little. Hence she was overjoyed when her parents proposed sending her to study art for two years in Munich itself. Her father, indeed, was disturbed by her lengthy youthful engagement to Karl Kollwitz. He knew that his Katuschen had great gifts, and felt sure she could have a career in art, but early marriage would prevent all that—or so he thought.

It worked out as Karl Schmidt had feared, in the case of his youngest daughter, Lise. She, too, clearly had great artistic gifts. In fact, her drawing won much praise, so much that Käthe, in spite of her love for Lise, felt jealousy, and later admitted it. Lise, however, did not devote herself to art after she married. Only the dogged determination and dedication of Käthe Kollwitz was triumphant over all distractions.

The Munich in which Käthe began life as an art student in 1888 excited and intoxicated her more than had Berlin. Munich was, after all, the true powerhouse in German art of that era. Furthermore, it had a noble tradition in graphics as well as in painting. There in 1806 Aloys Senefelder (1771–1834) had first operated the press that brought to the world his great new process called lithography, which he had perfected in 1800.

In Munich far more than Berlin the painting with light of the French Impressionists attracted attention and some followers. The bold experiments of the Impressionists were used as ammunition in a battle to "break free of the everlasting brown gravy of the studio." This statement referred to the dark colors and dull coats of varnish applied in the academic style of painting then prevalent in Germany.

The general level of art teaching in Munich was considered excellent. Even academic painters would agree that Munich's teaching surpassed that obtainable in Berlin. And for Käthe Schmidt who loved congenial people, companionship, and confidants, Munich offered one enormous and unfailing source of satisfaction: the art student life, with its camaraderie and *bonhomie*. Here were ease, relaxation, humor, pranks, and jokes both practical and verbal. Here were irreverent criticisms, eloquent spinning of new art theories, attacks, defenses, ripostes and refutations, gossip, and endless, eloquent talk. She felt delightfully at home among the youthful iconoclasts who were resisting, bending, and even breaking rigid academic rules which restricted the subjects for art and its handling of forms.

She found living quarters on Munich's Georgen Street and attended the School for Women Artists. Her principal teacher was the Munich painter Professor Ludwig Herterich, then only thirty-two years old. Unlike her Berlin teacher, Stauffer-Bern, he did not seek to concentrate her work on drawing. Perhaps less sensitive to Käthe's own tendencies or preferences, Herterich placed her in his regular painting class. Käthe at first considered his teaching to be stilted and his approach to art mannered and narrow. He had his own strongly marked ideas on all that concerned the use of color in painting. Käthe could not accept these ideas, though she kept her criticisms to herself. However, she did learn how to paint in the manner she knew he preferred. Thus Fräulein Schmidt from Königsberg remained among the art students on whom Herterich was pleased to lavish his personal attention.

She was sure, nevertheless, that the other students, even some who did not receive so much approval from Herterich, were gaining more from his instruction than she. She knew that they were basically more interested in color and more moved by it. Only later in life did she reach what she thought was an understanding of what Herterich had meant regarding the use of color. That was, however, long after she had decided to concentrate on graphic arts. She had chosen the road of black and white rather than color and never abandoned it.

She was still in Munich working under Herterich when the decisive event took place that crystallized her inclination toward graphics for her own work in art. One day she chanced to open a pamphlet entitled *Painting and Drawing*. Its author was the same Max Klinger whose etchings had so stirred and stimulated her in Berlin. Here Klinger had written a bold and eloquent defense of the pictorial methods other than painting—drawing and the graphic techniques. Some themes, Klinger declared, *should* be drawn rather than painted. They would be ineffective or even inartistic if rendered by means of painting. The graphic arts, he held, could better express the darker aspects of life. Thus they had their own roles, their own validity, their own justifications and were entitled equally with painting to be regarded as real art.

Käthe Schmidt read this avidly and repeatedly. It became for her a kind of Declaration of Independence. She realized that she was not at heart a painter. She never found cause later to change her mind. She did complete some paintings during the next years but only in an occasional and secondary way. Her heart belonged now to the art forms in which color was absent or, at most, subordinate: drawing and graphics.

Though her two years in Munich were much taken up with the problems of painting as taught by Herterich, Käthe did not feel that the time had been lost or wasted. It was under Herterich's training that she really learned, in her own words, "how to see." The work of her hands could begin, she realized, only when her eyes had ingested and digested the forms, the light, and shade that lay outside her. She ultimately concluded that she had been fortunate to have Herterich as a teacher, as she had been earlier to have Stauffer-Bern in Berlin.

Her Munich days were filled with work. She had, even then, the capacity for concentration that marked her long career in art. The evenings, however, brought friends and fun. Käthe went to dances, masquerades, beer cellars, picnics, and other outdoor excursions. It was wonderful to have her own house key and independence of action. Her good friend, Jeep, was also now in Munich as an art student, and their friendship continued.

There was a happy, adventurous excursion to Venice with Jeep and another woman art student. The girls had carefully saved money from their allowances and pooled it for the journey, which they managed to prolong beyond a week. In Venice they shared a room in a cheap lodging house where, much to her horror, during the first night, Käthe was badly bitten by bedbugs.

The days in Venice were gay. They could not afford to ride in gondolas, but wandered through the narrow streets, sailed on the *vaporetti* (public launches), and consumed spaghetti in cheap restaurants.

Back in Munich Käthe attended the Composition Club, which was open to both men and women students. It held evening meetings at which members' art works on various themes were shown and criticized. At one such session Käthe presented her charcoal study of a scene from *Germinal*, a powerful novel of coal miners by Émile Zola. She had drawn the smoke-filled interior of a tavern in which two men fought over a young girl. This study won great approval from Käthe's fellow students. She was so filled with joy

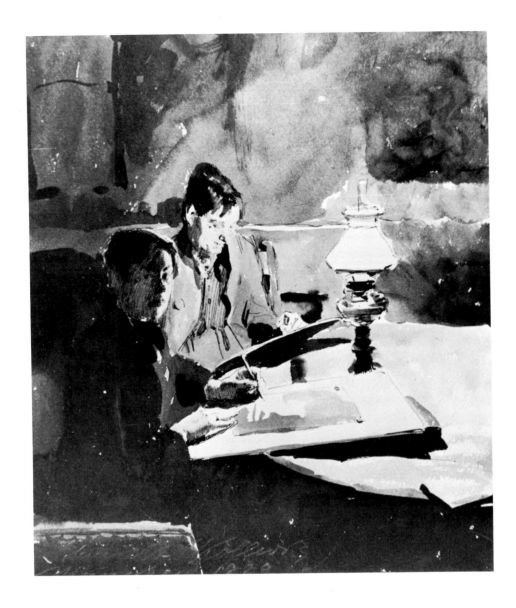

"Self-portrait at the Table,"
a pen and wash drawing made
while the artist was studying
in Munich. It is dated 1889
and signed by her with the
dual name "Schmidt-Kollwitz."
This has added weight to the
supposition that the young
man drawing beside her is her
fiancé Karl Kollwitz. However,
the artist's son, Dr. Hans
Kollwitz, has stated that it
does not depict his father as
a young man. In that case, it
may have been one of her
fellow art students in Munich.

This picture shows both
figures drawing left-handed.
She was right-handed, however.
This difference resulted because
she drew from a mirror image.
Galerie St. Etienne, New York.

and excitement that she could hardly sleep afterward. Wonderful visions of future triumphs filled her mind.

The great Naturalist writer Zola was not her only literary inspiration. In this period of expanding mental horizons she read works also by two provocative Norwegians: Henrik Ibsen and Björnstjerne Björnson (1832–1910). She attended lectures by social critics, reformers, and socialists and was especially impressed with *Women, Past, Present, and Future* by the socialist August Bebel (1840–1913). It increased her interest in feminism as well as in the socialism she already knew. Indeed, her later life became a triumphant example of how much a truly creative and liberated woman can contribute to the world.

During her time in Munich as well as the rest of her life Käthe found solace and strength in great music, and above all, in works by Bach and Beethoven. Munich was rich in music as well as pictorial art.

The freedom of an art student's life so appealed to her that she began to wonder whether she had been hasty in her engagement to Karl Kollwitz. After her first semester in Munich ended, her father offered her the choice between Munich and Berlin for the second year. She chose Munich readily.

Visiting Königsberg between semesters, she missed the gaieties of Munich. Also she admitted that she was not accomplishing much at home. "I can always paint very well with my eyes," she wrote, "but with my hands it doesn't always work out."

She was not alone in being dissatisfied with her progress. Her parents were not pleased with a portrait of Lise that she painted in this period. For a time there was even doubt as to whether she would be sent back to Munich after all. She felt relieved when permission finally was given.

Yet her second period of art study in Munich disappointed her. Later she regretted that she had not chosen Berlin, which was just beginning to develop into a major art center. Besides, her fiancé, Karl, had moved to Berlin for the half year of internship required before he could begin to practice medicine. Her brother, Konrad, was there too, now working on the staff of *Vorwärts*, the central newspaper of the Social Democratic Party. Berlin had become more attractive to Käthe than Munich.

By 1890 she was back again in Königsberg. Now she used the proceeds from the sale of "Before the Ball" to rent a tiny studio, "as big as a hand." Here she worked hard, basing many of her drawings on sights she had first seen and sketched during wanderings around the banks of the Pregel River. There were smoke-filled taverns and bars frequented by sailors and dock workers. The drunkenness, quarreling, fighting, and even knifings made her afraid to risk sketching after dark, but she would come by day to get details. The crooked streets and old buildings of the workers' districts enchanted her. Life in Munich had been merry and convivial, but now she could free herself from distractions and work alone, long and hard, a habit she never lost later.

She had still not given up painting entirely. There was a commission for a portrait. Also she wanted to paint that scene from Zola's *Germinal* which had won so much favor from her fellow art students in Munich. To do this, she found, she would need more instruction. She never underestimated her need to learn and never ceased to study for her art.

She persuaded her first teacher, Rudolph Mauer, to show her the basics of

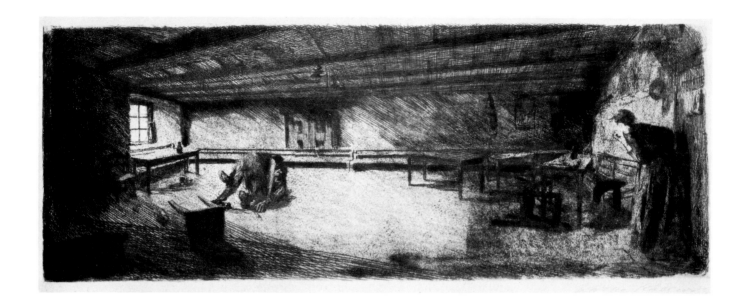

etching—how to coat and scratch the metal plate, how to mix and apply the biting acid. Though she had not the time for formal lessons, she was determined to learn at least the essentials of etching. She began in Königsberg and intended to continue in Berlin where she would soon be living after her marriage to Karl, which had been set for the month of June 1896.

Käthe began etching and made vast numbers of pen and ink exercises. It was rewarding work. She soon knew that though Herterich had helped her greatly, she had done more for herself in that one Königsberg winter of 1890–1891 than in all her months in Munich. In fact, the complete Klipstein catalogue of her graphic works shows three 1890 etchings, obviously done in Königsberg before her marriage, and revealing surprising skill. One plate contains a mélange of studies: heads, arms and hands, an ear, bottles, and so on. Another shows a young girl seated reading at a table with a glass of wine. The third is a female nude, seated. They are the promising beginnings of one of the truly great careers in etching, lithography, and woodcutting.

Karl Schmidt had hoped that by this time his daughter would have finished her preliminary art studies and begun to exhibit. Indeed, he doubted that she would in the future be able to make a success both of marriage and her art, and he told her so.

"You have chosen," said her concerned father, referring to her marriage.

"Scene from *Germinal*." (*Szene aus* Germinal) Etching, 1893.

The roots of this etching reach back to the artist's student days in Munich, when her composition won acclaim from fellow students. She intended to follow this etching with others, showing further scenes from Zola's novel—but gave up the project when she became committed to the theme of the weavers' uprising. *National Gallery of Art, Washington, D. C., Rosenwald Collection.*

"Be then wholly what you have chosen." But she did not follow his counsel to abandon her art and devote herself wholly to being a wife and mother. She chose rather to let no obstacle prevent her from going on with her work. Her lifelong belief in human rights, including the rights of women, underscored her determination to function successfully both as a creative artist and a wife.

Early in 1891 she wrote to a fellow art student in Munich mentioning that her coming marriage would endow her—as she jokingly put it—with the "stately" name of Kollwitz. Then more in earnest she told him how she had continued drawing and begun etching. After her marriage in Berlin there would be hardly any money to rent a studio. Oil painting in close quarters could be difficult. Etching, on the other hand, would be less troublesome.

She was not going to complete that scene from *Germinal* as a painting after all, but was making preliminary sketches in order to try it as an etching when she felt ready. Seemingly, practical problems, private preferences, and unconscious drives all combined to lead the purposeful Käthe finally and fully into the graphic media and away from painting.

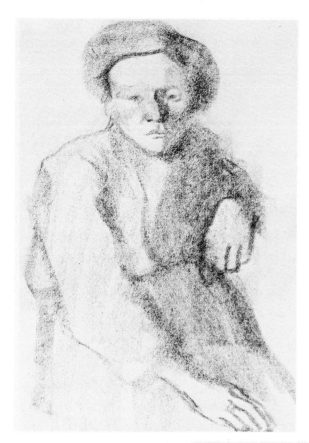

Drawing, charcoal or litho-
graphic crayon, about 1892.
   Frau Helene Wiess, seated.
*Collection of Dorothy Brown,
Malibu, California.*

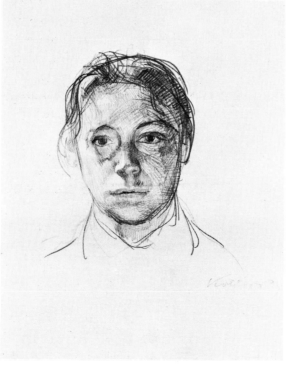

"Self-portrait," drawing in
pencil, about 1892.
   The newly married Frau
Käthe Kollwitz looked
into a mirror as she drew this—
one of the many unforgettable
depictions of her own face.
*Kupferstichkabinett, Dresden.
Photograph taken by
Deutsche Fotothek Dresden.*

chapter 3
1891-1899

Marriage, Berlin, and First Successes

Dr. Karl Kollwitz was appointed physician for a workers' health insurance fund, serving tailors and their dependents in the poor northeast section of Berlin. He and Käthe, married on his twenty-eighth birthday, June 13, 1891, moved into a third-floor apartment at 25 Weissenburger Street, near Wörther Place. It was a typical Berlin tenement—gray, somber, and damp. Yet here the new Frau Kollwitz was to reach the full flowering of her expression as a committed artist and produce some of the most moving and enduring graphic works of the last hundred years.

Karl Kollwitz was a dedicated physician, sensitive to his patients' needs and feelings. To him they were individual fellow human beings, not faceless cases or file numbers. His office was always crowded. There his wife saw sickness, unemployment, hunger, despair, children loved and children un-wanted—the whole bitter daily struggle to survive. In drawings and etchings she began to picture the sufferings, defeats, and endurance of the poor who came to her door.

At first in order to make proofs from the etched plates when they were inked, she applied pressure with a rolling pin from her kitchen. Later she acquired a small proofing press, and as she began to make larger etchings, she had to travel to the other side of Berlin to have a professional graphic printer pull her proofs.

Dr. Kollwitz earned little enough, but he did much to help his wife continue her art work. His own office was just downstairs from their flat. For years Käthe's studio was next to his office. Hers was a bare, modest workroom, far from the popular notion of an artist's atelier. A visitor found in it only sheer essentials: table, a press, a few chests of drawers containing the artist's prints and tools. None of her own drawings or prints decorated the walls. No flowers added color.

Outside in the hallway, silently seated against the walls, waited her husband's patients, many of whom became subjects of her drawings and prints. Only later did she have a studio away from the house where she and her husband lived all their long married life.

During the first years she continued to draw and worked for greater mastery in etching. Often she used the model most easily available—herself. In 1891 and 1892 she worked on her first etched self-portrait. More followed in 1893.

Whatever the subject, her style became increasingly distinctive. She eagerly studied other graphic artists but retained only what she felt could serve her and never followed the fads in art, whether they originated in Paris, Munich, or Berlin. She practiced neither art for art's sake nor escapism. With growing directness and concentration she made dramatic and revealing portrayals of the humble, the miserable, the helpless.

In the latter part of 1891, Käthe became pregnant. In May 1892 she was at work on an etching as the time for delivery approached. It was a sort of symbolic welcome to her first child, a tender, even joyous picture, "Greeting." Her labor pains, in fact, began as the plate lay in the acid bath. As a result, it remained longer than intended, accounting for the etching's unusually dark lines.

The Kollwitzes' first son was named Hans. Though now a mother as well as a wife, Käthe still took time to work on her art. She began experimenting with various methods for giving tone and texture to etchings, using soft ground and emery paper techniques. She also worked in aquatint—a medium beloved by Goya.

As she felt her mastery grow, she tried to exhibit her work. Time and again her submissions were turned down by juries whose tastes were academic and stilted. Then in 1893 she became part of an historic event in the art life of her city and land. The hidebound Association of Berlin Artists finally split up. A group of younger artists seceded from it and took independent action, staging their own exhibition as near as possible to the official show in the Hohenzollern Gallery.

To this show of the seceders young Frau Kollwitz contributed two pastels and one etching. Ludwig Pietsch, dean of establishment art critics in

"Greeting" (*Bergrüssung*) Etching, 1892.
This is the second and final state of the plate which played so special a role in the private life of the artist, being linked with the birth of her first son, Hans. The plate itself has been destroyed.
Kunsthalle, Hamburg.

"Self-portrait at the Table"
(*Selbstbildnis am Tisch*)
Etching and aquatint, 1893(?).
  This graphic work was the
second attempt; the first obviously did not satisfy the artist.
It is the second "state" of the
plate, which was printed in
three successive states or slight
variations.
Kunsthalle, Hamburg.

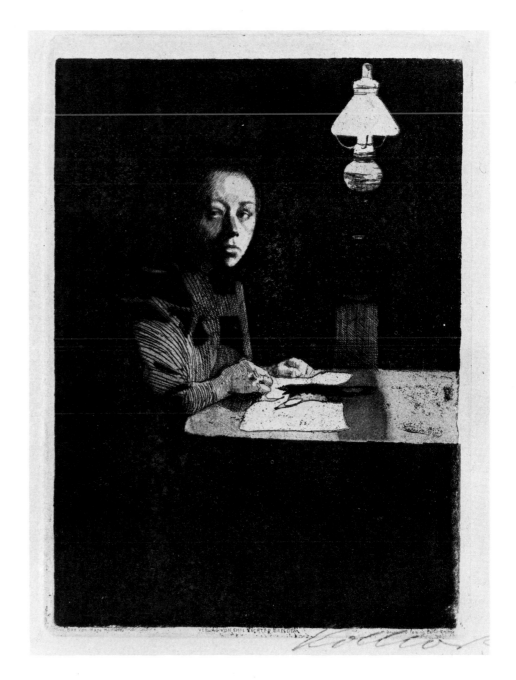

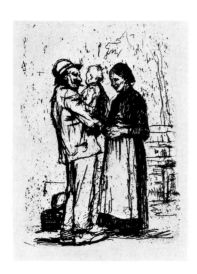

Berlin, reviewed the show unfavorably. He singled out Käthe's pictures, using as an antifeminist sneer, a quotation from *Faust* by her own beloved Goethe:

When the road leads to an evil place,
Woman has a head start in the race.

But another reviewer, Julius Elias, perceptively and prophetically praised her

29

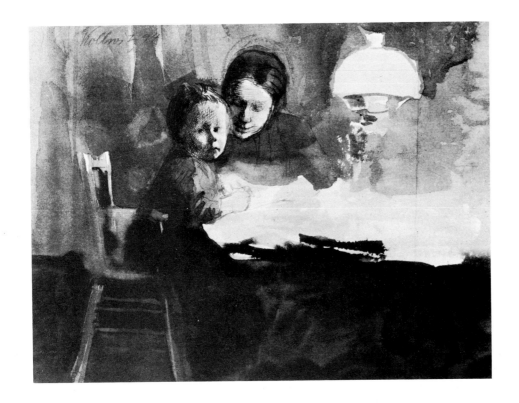

work, mentioning her "decisive talent," her simple yet intense response to
nature, and forecasting for her a "rich artistic future."

That future was linked for many years with the so-called Secessionist
movement, which followed the 1893 show. In fact, Secession came to be a
kind of catchall label in Berlin for every sort of militant, novel, or independent effort in the arts.

Year after year Käthe Kollwitz exhibited her best works at the Secession shows. She later accepted the Secession leaders' invitation to affiliate
with the group and remained with them for years until the time when, as
she put it, "they fell apart." By then they had largely attained their aim of
freeing German art from the deadening influence of rigid academic tradition.

Impressionism, mentioned earlier as a largely French school, was strong
in Germany during the first years of the Berlin Secession. Later, a more
dynamic and distortive approach called Expressionism came to the fore.
Finally, active Expressionists broke away and formed their own "New Secession," which also included groups of artists based in Dresden and Munich.

Käthe Kollwitz, however, cannot be classified either as an Impressionist
or Expressionist, though some expressionistic mood elements can be traced
in her later works. She said, in fact, that Expressionism was incomprehensible
to her. Its result, she felt, was merely "studio" art with eccentricities and
subtleties not understandable to the ordinary viewer. Affectation or obscurity

in art was alien to her purpose. She strove, then and later, for ever greater simplification and communication.

She continued deriving pictorial themes from her own life and reading. More than once a novel or play provided her with material. The years of activity as wife, mother, and untiring artist brought new depth and breadth to her work. This was apparent in the public showings that she now had regularly. Recognition could not long be denied this gifted and persistent artist, despite her preference for "controversial" or uncomfortable subjects.

On February 26, 1893, Gerhart Hauptmann's drama *The Weavers* was presented at a Berlin theater with a superb cast. It dramatized the desperation, revolt, and defeat of the Silesian weavers in 1844. Dr. Karl Kollwitz could not attend the performance—a morning affair—but his wife was there, eager and excited.

Nine years earlier the young girl from Königsberg had been enthralled by Hauptmann's reading from Shakespeare when she visited him at his home in Berlin. Now, *The Weavers* stirred her deeply. It even changed her plans for her work. She gave up the series she had already started on themes from Zola's *Germinal* and began work on the cycle now famous as *A Weavers' Uprising*.

Five years were devoted to completing this *Weavers* series. During that time, in 1896, her second son, Peter, was born. Other important prints, in-

"Portrait of Hans Kollwitz"
(*Bildnis von Hans Kollwitz*)
Lithograph, 1896.
This masterly picture was the artist's first published lithograph.
When it was completed she had made between twenty-five and thirty etchings. Hans, as shown here, was about four years old.
Deutsche Fotothek Dresden.

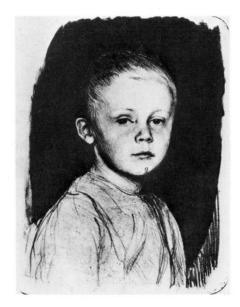

31

cluding self-portraits, were produced in this period also. All this was possible only because Käthe carefully budgeted her time and had a faithful housekeeper, Lina Mäkler, who remained with the family for more than fifty years, even helping to evacuate the residence during the bombings of World War II.

Käthe proved to herself and to her father that she could succeed as wife, as mother, and as artist too. Her home was neat, clean, and anything but bohemian. The work-filled day began early, when Käthe made plans with her housekeeper before going to the studio for hours of hard work. Nearly always she was at home when her sons returned from school.

Her successful completion of the extensive *Weavers* series and many other works was a tribute not only to her discipline as an artist, but also to the kindness, understanding, and cooperation of Karl Kollwitz. Their union was a firm and happy one. A friend has told how, even many years later when Karl was seventy and his wife in her late sixties, he would rise to his feet in greeting when she came into the room.

The relationship between Käthe and Karl Kollwitz was characterized not only by stability and loyalty but by deep mutual respect. Dr. Kollwitz would no more have dreamed of interposing his will or influence into her creative work than she would have sought to control or restrict his practice of medicine. Neither surrendered freedom or self-esteem to the other.

This becomes the more noteworthy when it is viewed against the background of typical family life in Germany at the time. Domination by the husband and father was taken almost for granted. Wives generally hesitated to express themselves without encouragement from their husbands. Fathers often dictated to children the way a drill sergeant might dictate to a new recruit. The Kollwitz household was fortunately atypical of its time and environment.

The individual self-reliance of Käthe Kollwitz as woman and artist was illustrated in her approach to the subject matter of her *Weavers* prints. She did not choose merely to illustrate Gerhart Hauptmann's drama. Instead thoughtfully and step by step she pictured essential highlights in a great historical tragedy. That uprising had been an explosion of desperate men and women ground down by a combination of aggressive new capitalism and decaying old feudalism. Their employers and overlords, seeking to meet the competition of machine-made British cloth, had borne down mercilessly on the handloom weavers of Silesia. The protest and brief revolt that followed was brutally crushed by Prussian soldiers.

The print cycle shows first, in "Poverty" (or "Misery"), the plight of the hungry weavers, resulting in "Death," which in turn moves them to "Conspiracy." They plan the "Weavers' March" in protest; this leads to "Attack" on the owners' fine mansions; and after the troops shoot them down comes the bitter "End."

The artist intended to etch all six subjects. The first three, though executed repeatedly in that medium, were finally completed as lithographs, for she still felt a lack of control in etching. The last three, however, she found herself able to handle as etchings. One can see that the first three—the lithographs—are somewhat more shadowy and mood-provoking; the final three are more pictorial and precise.

Completion of the series in 1898 was linked poignantly with her last contacts with her father. She had planned first to send him a copy of Heinrich Heine's great poem "The Weavers" as a birthday gift, then later to show him the full cycle of her six prints on the same subject. But news that he was seriously ill led her to hurry to him and give him all the prints. He was beside himself with joy. "They are good!" he cried. "You *can* do something." And ill as he was he ran through the house calling for his wife to come and see what their daughter Katuschen had made.

Karl Schmidt died the following March at the age of seventy-two. Käthe was so crushed to realize he could not see the *Weavers* prints displayed in public that she gave up the idea of offering them for exhibition. However, a good friend, Anna Plehn, insisted that she be allowed to handle the necessary technical arrangements. She registered the *Weavers* series and sent it to the jury. In 1898 it was displayed at the great Berlin Art Exhibit held at the Lehrter Railway Hall.

When a framed set of prints of the series was purchased for five hundred marks, the artist was open-mouthed with astonishment. "Isn't that fabulous?" she wrote to her friend Jeep.

The *Weavers* series caused a sensation, for it was one of the first times that powerful pictures had shown workers and their conflicts sympathetically. The show's jury, including famous artists old and young, nominated the *Weavers* cycle for a gold medal award.

The German monarch, Kaiser Wilhelm II, however, despised and feared art with this kind of social content. He called such works "gutter art." The

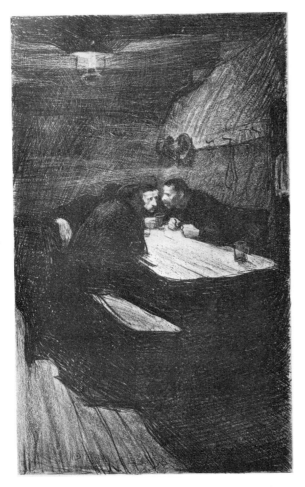

"Conspiracy" (*Beratung*) Lithograph, 1898. The third print from the *Weavers* series. *National Gallery of Art, Washington, D. C., Rosenwald Collection.*

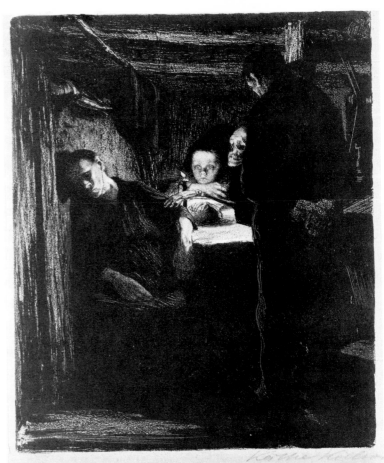

ABOVE:
"Death" (*Tod*) Lithograph, 1897. The second print from the *Weavers* series. Two major states of this print are known. This is an example of the second. The size is about 8½ x 7 inches. *Achenbach Foundation for Graphic Arts, California Palace of the Legion of Honor.*

OPPOSITE:
"End" (*Ende*) Etching, aquatint, and soft-ground, 1897. Sixth and last print in the *Weavers* series.

Here the soft-ground process produces the texture on the floor, walls, and clothing of the man who has just come through the door. *Achenbach Foundation for Graphic Arts, California Palace of the Legion of Honor.*

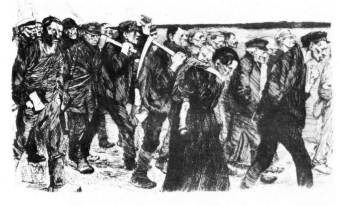

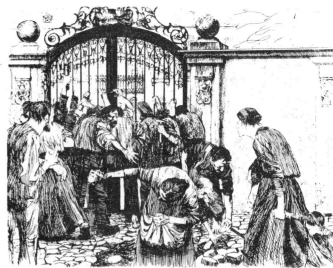

ABOVE:
"Weavers' March" (*Weberzug*)
Etching, 1897. Fourth print in
the *Weavers* series. Four states
of this etching are recorded;
this appears to be an example
of the first.
Staatliche Museen zu Berlin.

ABOVE:
"Attack" (*Sturm*) Etching and
soft-ground, 1897. Fifth print
in the *Weavers* series.

The artist also used here
the soft-ground texture
producing process known in
German as *Schmirgeldruck-
verfahren*. Such texture can be
seen on the wall, and also on
the backs of the four figures
standing by the iron gate.
Kupferstichkabinett, Dresden.
Photograph taken by
Deutsche Fotothek Dresden.

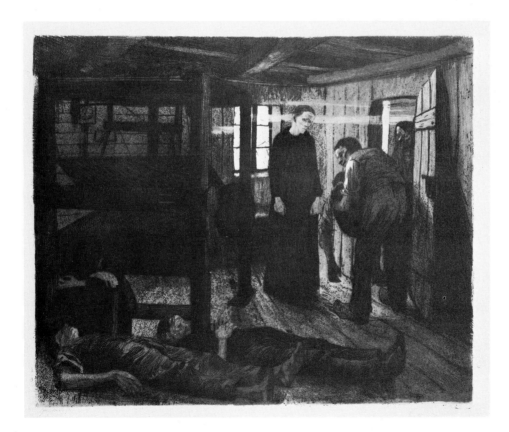

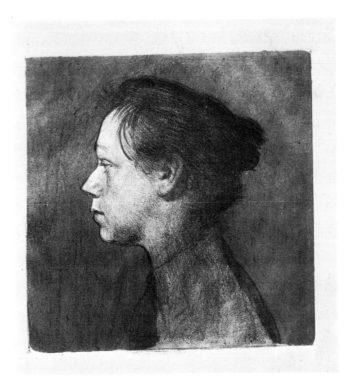

"Self-portrait in Profile, Facing Left" (*Selbstbildnis im Profil nach Links*) Lithograph, 1898. This is the second and final state of the lithograph. *Staatliche Museen zu Berlin.*

award was blocked by his veto. A third of a century later, Adolf Hitler played a similar but even more devastating role in opposition to the art of Käthe Kollwitz and others.

Berlin's rapidly growing art public was not completely swayed by the kaiser's disapproval. The *Weavers* cycle was studied, discussed, praised, and recommended by word of mouth. The next year, Max Lehrs purchased the series for the Dresden Museum print collection, of which he was then the head. Exhibited in Dresden that same year the series won the gold medal. In 1900 it also won a prize at a London exhibition. From then on, Käthe Kollwitz belonged among the foremost graphic artists of her era.

Subsequently, Lehrs was brought from Dresden to head the great Berlin Museum print collection. In his new post, as in the earlier one, he acquired for the museum many great prints by Kollwitz.

In the *Weavers* cycle and important later works, Käthe Kollwitz departed significantly from the practice of many earlier artists such as Goya and Daumier (1808–1879). They had shown the oppressors as well as the oppressed in social conflicts. She, however, almost never pictured the oppressors. In none of the *Weavers* prints do the employers or the kaiser's troops appear. Only in "Attack" do we even glimpse the elegant gates of the owners' mansion. All is seen in terms of the workers and from their viewpoint. It is an art of those at the bottom. The workers appear as products of their

LEFT:

"Downtrodden Ones" (*Zertretene*) Etching, 1900.

This originally formed the left-hand quarter of a vertical etching, about 9 ⅜ × 32 ¾ inches in size. Several printings were made from the entire plate, which was then divided, and this portion published separately. *Kunsthalle, Hamburg.*

RIGHT:

"Head of Child and Hands of Mother" Pencil study for the lower portion of the etching "Downtrodden Ones" (*Zertretene*), 1900.

In this drawing, the child's head is inclined to the right, but in the completed etching, because of the reversal of the printing process, the head is inclined to the left. The original drawing was about 8¼ × 8¼ inches. *Kupferstichkabinett, Dresden. Photograph taken by Deutsche Fotothek Dresden.*

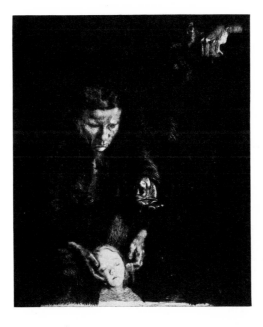 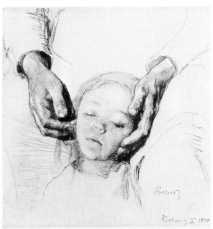

miserable lives. We see their dejection and their defiance. Their bodies bear evidence of bad nutrition and unhealthy working conditions.

Käthe had intended a cycle of seven, not six, prints. In fact, she did make the seventh—an elaborate and highly allegorical etching entitled "Oh People, You Bleed from Many Wounds." However Julius Elias, her sympathetic critic, persuaded her to omit it from the *Weavers* series. The deleted print remains a fascinating example of the sort of thing she finally outgrew. Unlike the best of her work, it is mystically symbolic, reminiscent of much of Max Klinger. She had learned a great deal from his masterly techniques, but she finally rejected his symbolism, drenched as it was in sentiment and vague allusions.

In 1900 in an etching "Downtrodden Ones," she again seems to have been tempted by mystical allegory but later came to regard that work also as too sentimental and not quite a success. An etching of 1899, "Revolt," shows a marching group of infuriated workers, urged onward by a symbolic female figure floating in the sky. But after the turn of the century she seems to have rid herself of all traces of Klinger-like symbolism and established her individual style.

One might ask whether symbolism recurs in the series of eight drawings published in 1924 under the title of *Parting and Death*, or again in her final series of eight lithographs called simply *Death*, completed in 1934 and 1935, early in the Hitler era. However, in these, Death, whether personified as a friend or a foe, is made stark, realistic, and overpowering, not vaguely or romantically symbolic in the Klinger fashion.

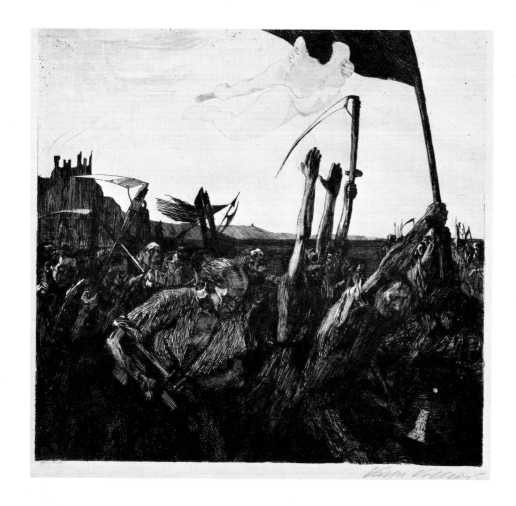

As early as 1899, on seeing some of Klinger's sculptures exhibited in Dresden, Käthe Kollwitz had felt great disappointment. They appealed to her far less than his best etchings. At the same time, however, she had been quite overcome by a memorial to the dead sculpted by the French artist Paul Bartholomé (1848–1928). She found it "shatteringly beautiful and big and simple."

She pronounced paintings by the Spanish artist Ignacio Zuloaga (1870–1945) "fine," a word she used often to express her ready enthusiasms.

Something quite different also evoked her enthusiasm as well as her love of fun. Jeep had sent her a book called *Stories of Painters*, published in Leipzig. It contained anecdotes and tales from the world of art students and artists. Jeep herself had supplied some of them.

"I'm still laughing," Schmidt wrote to Jeep. "Our whole time in Munich came to life for me. Had you been at hand, I'd have hugged you for delight . . . the things are fabulously told and sometimes are so funny that I threw back my head and roared aloud with laughter."

chapter 4
1899-1908

The "Socialist Artist" in Paris, Florence, and the World

"Socialist artist" was the label often applied to Käthe Kollwitz after her *Weavers* prints became known. However, her own view, stated some time later, was different. It was true, she wrote, that she had been moved toward socialism by the influences of her father, her brother, and literature—and that compassion and pity played their parts. But there was another reason why she chose workers' lives and struggles for her subjects. Those themes seemed to her simpler, freer, fuller. She found the workers—their bodies, motions, and expressions—meaningful and beautiful, too. In the proletariat she found great scope and stimulus. The bourgeois and well-to-do, on the contrary, did not attract her. They seemed dull, stiff, uninteresting.

Working women, she discovered, disclosed their feelings far more than did middle-class women. She found meaning and importance in the hands, feet, and hair of the workers, and the suggestions of physical form beneath their clothing. The bodies shaped by labor remained beautiful to her. *Le beau c'est le laid*, she quoted. "Beauty is that which is ugly."

At first the workers around her in Berlin seemed less attractive than those in Königsberg. The Berlin workers were quite different, seemingly on a higher level of awareness, but outwardly less appealing. Sometimes she wished she had stayed longer in East Prussia to get from workers there all that they offered for her art. However, she became involved more and more with the plight of the workers who came as patients to her husband. Many of the women who visited Dr. Kollwitz came to her as well. She found some release from her deep personal concerns with social problems in her many portrayals of the lives of these afflicted people, indeed, "a way to endure life."

The success of her *Weavers* prints brought her her first teaching assignments: instruction in graphics and drawing from live models at the Berlin School for Women Artists. She feared that she knew too little of etching methods to fill such a post. However, she became a good teacher then as well as later in the graphics master class she conducted from 1928 to 1933. She encouraged her students to be free in approaching their material, to see fully before they drew, and she helped them as individuals as well as future artists. Her most constant message was that they think in terms of large masses rather than incidental details—in other words, to set down the forest, not the separate trees.

The usual academic approach at that time was still to follow likeness faithfully. She thought this attitude was slavish. Advising a young artist in 1915 she urged: begin with thorough study of the model or object, note its details, but go after its essentials. Do not, she warned, look constantly from model to paper, but train the visual memory by drawing the dominant impression from recollection only. Afterward, compare the drawing with the original object.

She stressed clear and emphatic contrasts. "Separate the light from the darkness," she told even her early students. In her teaching, as in her own work, she tended to reduce intermediate gray tones, to attain sharp, bold division of black and white, to omit small, distracting detail. More and more, she moved toward large masses, simpler figures, bolder areas of light and dark.

Sometimes she has been called academic, for she was faithful to the human form and not attracted by Impressionistic vagueness or Expressionistic distortions. Yet as a teacher she seemed unacademic. She shared her artistic insights in many ways—teaching in classes, personally advising and aiding younger artists, and responding to requests to evaluate work submitted by many beginners whom she never met face to face. She seemed unable to say no to such appeals. When she could she gave encouragement as well as counsel.

Constantly she stressed that art should grip, even shatter, the human heart. Her approach to those who sought to advance in art was similarly heartfelt. Though she was reserved and laconic about all that concerned herself, she could not be a cold, objective critic of the work of the young. Both she and her husband were by nature givers. Old and young came constantly to them with problems by no means limited to artistic matters. The

Kollwitzes were patient, sympathetic listeners. Often they gave financial and material as well as emotional help.

The artist valued and protected her own working time but did not divorce what was hers from what she shared with her students and protégés. Thus she once gave a young artist her own copy of *The Art of Etching* by Börner, a work she had used for many years as a kind of encyclopedia of techniques. The visitor hesitated to accept it. What if Frau Kollwitz herself should have need of it again? "Then you can lend it to me sometime," was the answer.

Käthe Kollwitz was hard and unyielding, however, in one important respect. She had no mercy for those who were willing to compromise or sell out their talents. In the drawings of one younger woman she easily detected the effects of doing commercial art jobs for a newspaper. "One can see it . . . ," she warned. "If you don't stop, you will spoil your art work for all time."

If an artist had to earn a living while learning, far better to address envelopes or do any other kind of labor that had nothing to do with art, she advised.

Käthe Kollwitz influenced younger artists principally by personal contacts in or out of classes rather than by writing texts and formal rules. In her teaching and counseling she used personal comments and the influence of her personality as well as examples drawn from her own works. Even while she taught others she continued to study for the sake of her own art. By the early 1900s she had tried a host of variations in etching techniques, including aquatint, drypoint, and soft-ground methods. She even worked with a combination of metal plate and lithographic stone, a hybrid litho-etching.

Among the methods she explored were: (a) drawing with pen and ink on a copper plate, then covering the plate with a soft ground (varnish) and immersing it in water, thus removing the ground from the inked areas; (b) sprinkling sand on the soft ground, thereby making indentations that the acid would attack; (c) pressing thin, fine-textured fabrics into the ground; (d) using emery paper backing for the transfer paper on which she drew her lithographic designs.

The etching "Dance around the Guillotine," or "Carmagnole," shown at the 1901 Secession exhibition, added to her fame. Its subject is reminiscent of Dickens' *Tale of Two Cities*, though it has been said that here the French

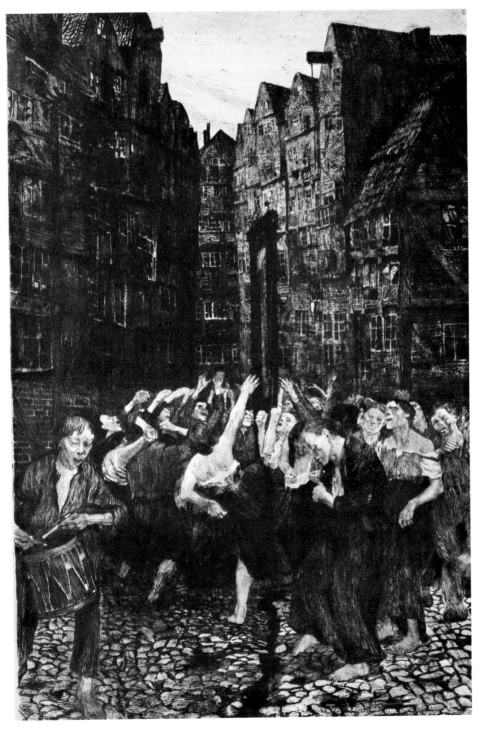

"Carmagnole," or "Dance around the Guillotine" (*Die Carmagnole*) Etching and aquatint, with soft-ground texture process, 1901.

The "Carmagnole" was one of the popular songs of the French Revolution in 1792 and included the verse: "Dansons la Carmagnole, / Vive le son du canon." ("Let us dance the Carmagnole, / Long live the sound of the cannon.") *National Gallery of Art, Washington, D. C., Rosenwald Collection.*

revolutionaries look more like proletarians of the artist's own time than like Parisians of the late eighteenth century.

The next year she began work on another great series, *Peasants' War*, inspired as before by history, literature, her memories, and her imagination. The actual Peasants' War had been a great but unsuccessful struggle against serfdom and feudalism during the time of the Reformation. The peasants' revolts were bloodily crushed in most areas by 1525.

"Outbreak," the best-known print of the cycle, was completed in 1903. This etching alone decided the Society for Historical Art to commission the entire series, in which "Outbreak" became the fifth of seven scenes. Completed in 1908 the seven prints were distributed to members of the Society.

As children, the artist and her brother, Konrad, had played at being peasant revolutionaries on imaginary barricades. Since then, she had been deeply stirred by the figure of Black Anna, a leader who summoned the peasants to rise against their oppressors. It is Black Anna—with whom the artist identified herself—who stands with upraised arms urging the rebels onward in "Outbreak." This earthy, active, powerful figure contrasts sharply with the idealized and unreal female figure—pure allegory—pictured hovering over the marchers in "Revolt," only four years earlier.

"Sleeping Boy" (*Schlafender Knabe*) Study in pencil and crayon, heightened with white, 1903.

The boy is probably her older son, Hans, then ten or eleven.

The artist joined together two pieces of paper, the strip at the right being darker than the piece at left.
Staatliche Museen zu Berlin.

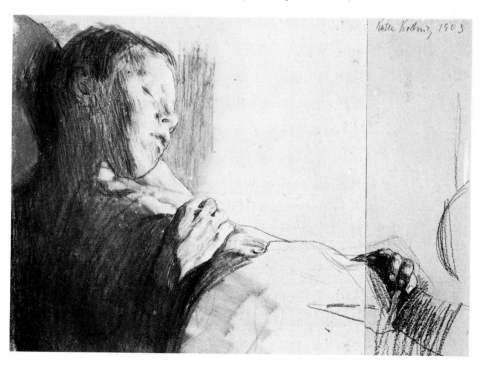

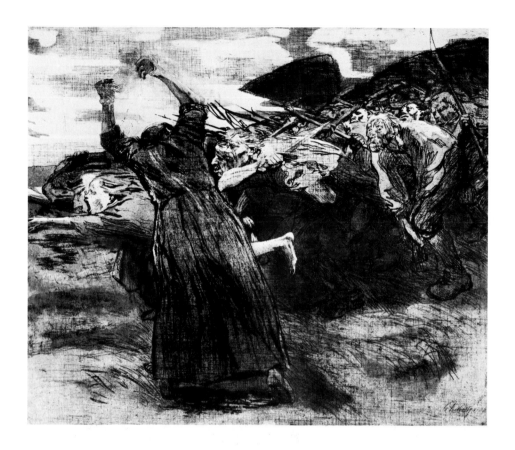

"Outbreak" (*Losbruch*)
Etching, 1903.

This became the fifth of the seven prints in the series known as the *Peasants' War* (*Bauernkrieg*). No less than eleven different states of the plate are recorded, of which this is the sixth. The size of the original plate was about 19⅞ × 23 inches.

The artist reworked the upraised hands of the Black Anna figure at left, producing the cloudlike effect around them.

Staatliche Museen zu Berlin.

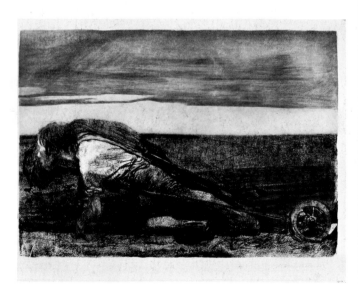

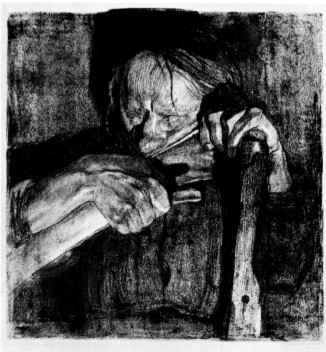

"Battlefield" (*Schlachtfeld*)
Etching and press-through
process, 1907. The sixth
print in the *Peasants' War* series.
  The smooth tone imparted by
the press-through process
in the dark night sky is apparent
here. Though imposed on a
metal plate worked in acid,
such processes in the skillful
hands of the artist rivaled
effects obtained on the lithographic stone.
Kunsthalle, Hamburg.

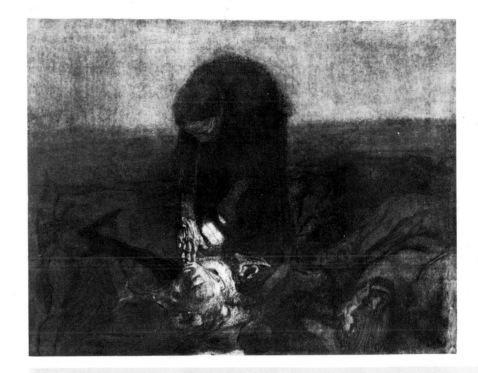

"The Prisoners" (*Die
Gefangenen*) Etching and
press-through process, 1908.
The seventh and final print of
the *Peasants' War* series.
Kunsthalle, Hamburg.

"The Plowers" (*Die Pflüger*)
Etching and aquatint, 1906. The
first of the seven prints in the
Peasants' War series.
Kunsthalle, Hamburg.

"While Sharpening the Scythe"
(*Beim Dengeln*) Etching, with
"press-through process,"
1905. The third of the prints
in the *Peasants' War* series.
Kunsthalle, Hamburg.

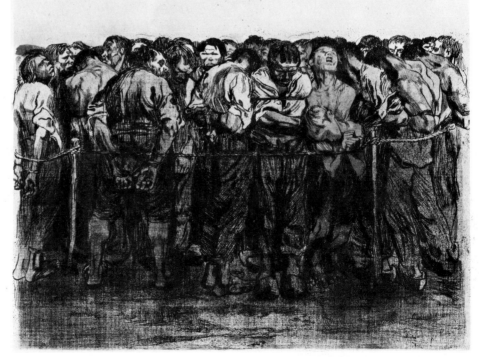

The seven *Peasants' War* prints are: "The Plowers," showing the bestial enslavement of the peasants; "Raped," depicting one of many outrages perpetrated by their masters; "While Sharpening the Scythe," suggesting the mounting resentment; "Arming in the Vault," the prelude to open resistance; "Outbreak," already noted; "Battlefield," the aftermath for the dead peasant fighters; and "The Prisoners," captured survivors who are still defiant as they await torture or execution.

Incidentally, "Raped" is the only graphic work of the artist that shows flowers or shrubbery. She deeply loved nature and was soothed by it but created no landscapes or even any still lifes. Human beings were her only subjects.

During her years of work on the *Peasants' War* series she made and discarded many plates before completing the set that met her high standards. At first she made lithographic studies but finally chose etching as the only medium for this particular series. In these *Peasants' War* prints her human figures appear larger, more massive. They were to become even more so in the years ahead.

While she completed the *Peasants' War* cycle, she created also many other major works, including self-portraits. Her experiments in graphic media and effects continued.

As she worked on a preparatory drawing for a 1903 etching, "Woman with Dead Child," she posed before a mirror with her younger son, Peter, then about seven. In the effort of holding him across her lap while working, she groaned, but he told her, "Be quiet, Mother, it is going to be very beautiful." Later in life, she was to call this etching prophetic.

The years between her thirtieth and fortieth birthdays were happy ones for Käthe Kollwitz. She was artistically productive, her children were growing well, the family had all it needed to live on. Together they went on many outings and did much traveling. The artist was still an enthusiastic walker and hiker of great endurance.

The social life of the Kollwitzes was devoted to personal friendships rather than to the advancement of an artistic career. Karl Kollwitz was busy with his medical practice. His professional contacts and those of his artist wife were different. For a number of years while the children were small there was open house every Thursday evening; artists, students, literary people, Russian emigrés, and strangers visited the Kollwitz home.

Even after these Thursday evenings were given up, many visitors still

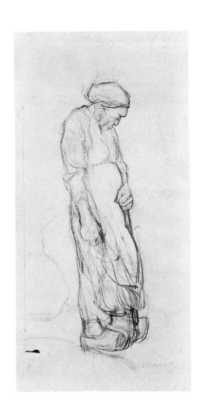

"Standing Woman" (*Stehende Frau*) Pencil study, 1905.

The heavy wooden shoes suggest, not that this woman comes from the Netherlands, but that she does some sort of damp or wet labor in Berlin where the artist sketched her. *National Gallery of Art, Washington, D.C., Rosenwald Collection.*

came to the artist in her home or studio. She was constantly sought out as a sympathetic listener and helper for friends and acquaintances in distress. Young people were often among the guests who stayed a night or two in the Kollwitz extra room.

Käthe Kollwitz followed the literature and art of France as well as Germany. She had read widely in Zola, Balzac, Hugo (1802–1885), and Baudelaire (1821–1867). Many French artists appealed to her, especially Daumier, Maillol (1861–1944), Toulouse-Lautrec (1864–1901), and the sculptor Rodin (1840–1917).

In 1904 Käthe Kollwitz visited Paris for a number of weeks, and saturated herself with memorable art experiences. In the mornings she attended sculpture classes at the Julian Academy. Afternoons and evenings she devoted to museums, to the Montmarte dance halls, to markets, cellars, and bohemian hangouts on the Boulevard Montparnasse. She met artists, writers, critics, and thinkers. Twice she made unforgettable visits to the great sculptor Auguste Rodin, once at his residence in Meudon, once at his studio. In Meudon Käthe saw memorable Rodin sculptures, including his "Balzac," a powerful masterpiece, and also small model statues executed in plaster of Paris. Many years later she was to turn to sculpture as her own final choice among the many art media that she mastered.

She also made a studio visit to Théophile-Alexandre Steinlen (1859–1923), a great, Swiss-born, satirical graphic artist. He too had been impelled to portray and identify with the poor, and some art critics state that his work definitely influenced hers. The liveliness of Steinlen and his family delighted the artist from Berlin.

Paris so enthralled her that she gave up plans to return to Berlin by way of Brussels. There she had hoped to visit the sculptor Constantin Meunier (1831–1905), a veteran portrayer of workers in the style called Social Realism. Meunier died soon afterward, so the two never met.

Though she herself did not meet Meunier, her work reached him during the last years of his life. The eminent German art scholar and museum director Max Lehrs visited Meunier, then in his seventies, and showed him some prints by Kollwitz. The aged Belgian master looked at them long and hard. Finally he broke his silence. "Never before have I seen such work by a woman!"

He did not mean this as faint praise (though today it may have overtones of condescension). The handicaps imposed on artists who happened to be women were many. Kollwitz herself was well aware of them, then and later. In those days and for years afterward art dealers often allowed only initials instead of full signatures to appear on prints or paintings by women artists. Many customers would not willingly pay as much for a work if they knew the artist to be a woman.

In a work on modern graphics published in 1920, H. W. Singer said that it had been important to Käthe Kollwitz to dispel or resist this prejudice. In fact, Singer suggested that her awareness of it led her to try too hard in her own work. He implied that in her prints she purposely made her points more strongly than she might have done had there been no anti-feminist prejudice.

The struggle for real equality in the treatment accorded all artists, women or men, is far from over in the 1970s. However, undeniable progress can be seen. A statement today such as "Kollwitz did fine work, considering that she was [only?] a woman," would be widely regarded as evidence of insensitivity to art as well as human values. The full body of Kollwitz's work is outstanding proof that art, in any medium, must be judged for itself and not according to the sex of the artist.

Following Käthe's return from Paris, the Kollwitz household gained a new member—Georg Gretor, a boy of twelve, just the age of her elder son, Hans. While in Paris she had found Georg living there in bitter poverty. His mother, a fellow art student of Käthe's in the Munich days, was with him but unable to pay much attention to him. Touched by his plight, Käthe arranged for him to come to Berlin and live with her family. He stayed with them for many years, treated as lovingly as a son.

Recognition began to come to the artist in various forms. A guidebook, *Berlin and the Berliners*, published in 1905 included her among principal artists of the capital city, giving her address, listing her series on the *Weavers* and *Peasants' War*, and mentioning her "distinguished treatment of social material."

In 1905 she lithographed a drawing for a poster on behalf of the Home Industries exhibition held the next year to aid those very poor whose meager living was earned in their own homes.

The kaiserin, wife of Emperor Wilhelm II, was supposed to be sympathetic to the cause of the home workers. But like her military-minded husband, she disapproved of the art of this "socialist," Frau Kollwitz. Her majesty let it be known that she would not visit the exhibition until the Kollwitz

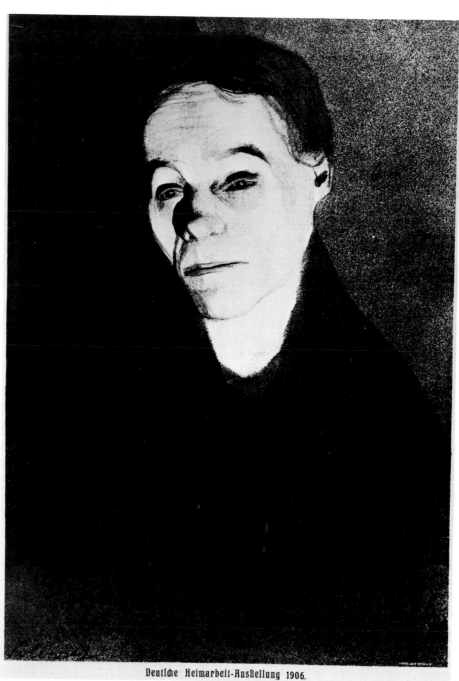

Deutsche Heimarbeit-Ausstellung 1906.

Poster for the Home Industries Exhibit (*Plakat der deutschen Heimarbeit-Ausstellung*) Lithograph, 1905. This is the second of three states of this subject. The original is about 27 × 19⅛ inches.

In a later modification, this lithograph was combined with a text announcing an exhibit on behalf of the home industries workers. This is an early example of the many posters which the artist created so effectively. *Staatliche Museen zu Berlin.*

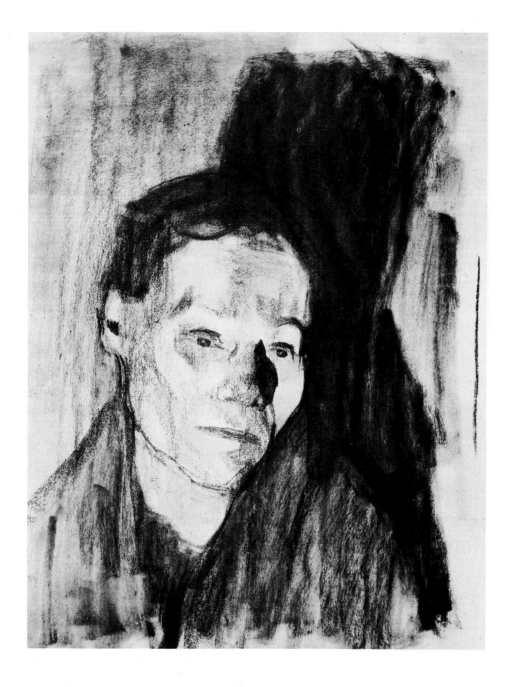

poster was removed. Later, in 1909, the artist did a charcoal drawing, "Home Work," which dealt with the same bitter problems.

The *Peasants' War* series brought her a substantial honor. In 1907 she was awarded the Villa Romana Prize, founded by Max Klinger himself. It gave her up to a year of art study in Italy with expenses paid. A fine studio and residence in the Villa Romana in Florence was placed at her disposal, but she did no work there. She would have preferred to have the same length of time in Paris. At first her younger son, Peter, was with her. However, he soon returned to Berlin with his father, who had come to Florence only for a visit.

During her stay in Florence she "pilgrimaged" through all the churches and monasteries. Her days were also filled with trips to art galleries, museums, and architectural treasures. The artist responded most strongly to the drama and vigor of Masaccio (1401–1428?), the lyricism of Donatello (1386?–1466), and the powerful sculptures of Michelangelo (1475–1564). Her home afterward was decorated by two huge photographs, one of Michelangelo's "Night" from the Medici tomb, the other of his "Moses" in Rome. Botticelli (1444?–1510), many of whose canvases are in the Uffizi Gallery, left her with mixed feelings. On the one hand, she found some figures in his paintings wonderful in conception, color, and draftsmanship, but others seemed to her decadent, stupid, and affected.

Some of the individuals then in Florence soon absorbed her more than did the masterworks in the museums and churches. Her art school friend Jeep lived near the city with her husband, Arthur Bonus, a writer on

"Home Worker" (*Heimarbei-terin*) Charcoal drawing, 1909. The size of the original, about 16 × 22¼ inches.

In this drawing, the artist returned again to the plight of those most exploited and unprotected of Germany's workers—pieceworkers—mainly women, who labored long hours in their homes or hovels, until overcome by fatigue or illness.
Los Angeles County Museum of Art, Graphic Arts Council Fund.

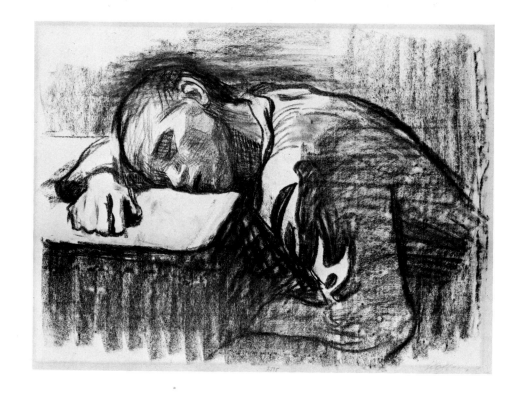

religious subjects. Jeep had lived much in Italy as a girl before she met Käthe Schmidt. Now the Bonuses were glad to have their good friend near for a time.

In sharp contrast to the quiet and conventional-minded Bonus couple was Stan, a striking and free-spirited young English girl with whom Käthe became closely acquainted. Stan's background and life-style were unusual indeed for 1907. She had been Constanza Harding, daughter of a British professional teataster who traveled much in Europe, taking his two children along and dominating their lives. When she reached twenty, Constanza rebelled and struck out for herself, remaining in Florence while her father and brother traveled elsewhere. She had no money and nearly starved while she developed her self-taught skill: copying masterpieces in the Uffizi.

She was slender and intense, with hair cut shockingly short in what was later known as pageboy style. She even cut her name to Stan as a time-saving measure. Her plight stirred the compassion of a German doctor named Krayl who was practicing there, his patients mostly tourists and visitors from Germany, England, and the United States. Stan moved into his house. Now she ate regularly and had shelter. Her doctor-protector was able to find buyers for her copies of masterpieces, thus assuring her some income.

Soon the proprieties required that they go through a marriage ceremony, though this was more for the sake of the doctor's standing than to satisfy the wishes of Stan, who always wanted full freedom to come and go as she pleased. Even after she became Stan Harding-Krayl, she did not become domesticated. She tramped alone through streets and byways as impulse moved her. To protect herself she secured a license to carry a pistol, which she did not hesitate to produce and point if she felt menaced.

Between this girl of barely twenty and the great German artist of almost forty an unmistakable attraction developed. Käthe again showed herself in her unsought role as mother confessor to troubled people. Both Stan and Dr. Krayl came to reveal to her their complaints or self-defenses about the unsatisfying nature of their "marriage." Käthe Kollwitz listened much but was wise enough to offer little advice.

Beside their different involvements in art, Stan and Käthe were linked also by another shared enthusiasm. Both loved to travel long distances on foot. They were enormous walkers. While an art student in Munich a score of years before, Käthe had been admiringly compared to a chamois—a nimble mountain antelope—because of her vigor in climbing the Bavarian hills and mountains. This praise pleased her, for she relished this physical freedom and loved the outdoors even though in her art she concerned herself not with landscapes or vistas but always with people.

Käthe's plan was to move on to Rome for a time and there meet her son Hans, who was coming to Italy for some weeks of summer vacation before they returned to Berlin together. She and Stan decided to take a walking tour all the way from Florence south to Rome. The point-to-point distance was about 150 miles, but the route they chose was at least double that. They set out, walking mostly at night and resting during the insufferable heat of the Italian summer days.

Peasants and villagers who saw this unusual pair generally assumed that they were mother and daughter. Also, it was often thought that they must be penitents making a pilgrimage on foot to the Vatican and that substantial sins must have required so energetic an act of atonement! A hike to Rome by two women alone constituted a real conversation piece in the countryside.

Käthe Kollwitz found this long foot journey fascinating. As she and Stan approached the great Roman Campagna, they became impatient and walked most of the last two nights as well as days, trying without success to hitch rides on passing wagons. They made their footsore entry into the Eternal City on June fifteenth. Stan was still relatively lively, but Käthe was so exhausted that she had to rest in bed for a couple of days. However, she recovered in time to begin touring Rome and then to greet her son, Hans, who arrived from Berlin all by himself, quite proud of his fifteen-year-old self-reliance.

Mother and son saw many of the great sights of Rome, then went north to Florence and Spezia where they met Karl Kollwitz, newly arrived from Berlin with young Peter. The four were rowed to a tiny fishing settlement called Fiascherino on the Ligurian Sea where they lived in rooms rented from fisherfolk. After a while they were joined by Stan and her husband. Somehow, all six of them found room enough, enjoyed the swimming and diving, and "lived the most splendid weeks of vacation." In that summer Käthe turned forty, "lean and brown from the sun and the sea."

Their return to gray Berlin was hastened by alarming news. Käthe's dear sister and intimate, Lise Stern, now in her late thirties, was about to give birth to her fourth child, and it was proving a most difficult and dangerous ordeal.

However, by the time Käthe and her family reached Berlin, they found the baby had been born, and both mother and infant doing rather well. This fourth Stern daughter was named Maria. Käthe's four nieces, the Stern girls, were all quite close to her and their Uncle Karl and were notably talented, musically and dramatically. Their father, Georg Stern, though an industrialist and engineer by profession, was a fine pianist and composer by avocation. His daughters sang beautifully and naturally in chorus or solo from their earliest youth.

The three elder Stern girls teamed with the theater-loving Hans Kollwitz to enact plays for their parents' and their own satisfaction. Some of the dramas were written by Hans himself, who had dreams then of becoming a playwright-actor. On one very special occasion they presented a performance of Maxim Gorki's great study of human poverty and degradation, *The Lower Depths*; on another, it was Hugo von Hofmannsthal's (1874–1929) *The Fool and Death*; on still another, Schiller's melodramatic *Cabal and Love*.

The principals in these casts were Hans and Peter Kollwitz, Georg Gretor, who lived with and was like a brother to them, and their two older cousins, Regula and Hanna Stern. Since some of the plays in their repertory had more roles than they could handle, they allowed their parents to fill in.

It was typical of Käthe's involvement in the enthusiasms of the young as well as her continuing dedication to drama and human emotion that, for the final gala family performance of *The Lower Depths*, she found time to learn all her lines by heart, and allowed her house "to be turned upside down."

It was her niece Regula, eldest of the four Stern girls, who first sought and found success on the stage. Regula, however, decided after a time in favor of a career in medicine; but she died while still relatively young. The second girl, Hanna, became an excellent actress under the stage name of Hannah Hofer. She married an energetic, aggressive actor-director, Fritz Kortner, who was well known on the German stage and screen. The third daughter, Katta, inspired by the Russian ballerina, Pavlova, became a superb dancer. The youngest, Maria, also became a dancer under the name of Maria Solveg. Later, as Maria Matray, she became a successful dramatic writer for radio and television, and in 1970 co-authored her first published book. Both Hanna and Maria spent many years in the United States during Hitler's rule of Germany.

In the years following her first artistic successes articles about Käthe

Kollwitz had appeared in various German periodicals, but it was 1908, the year in which she turned forty-one, that brought the publication of the first book devoted entirely to her art. The author, H. W. Singer, included reproductions of her work with his descriptive and critical text. This book was the first of a number of others in German, and a few in English, dealing with the growing body of graphic art from this seemingly tireless creator.

The artist herself about this time began a different kind of book, her "tagebuch," or diary. She was to continue making entries—fascinating, pithy, penetratingly honest—at frequent intervals for the next thirty-five years. The final entry, in fact, was made amid the alarms and terrors of war-torn Berlin in 1943.

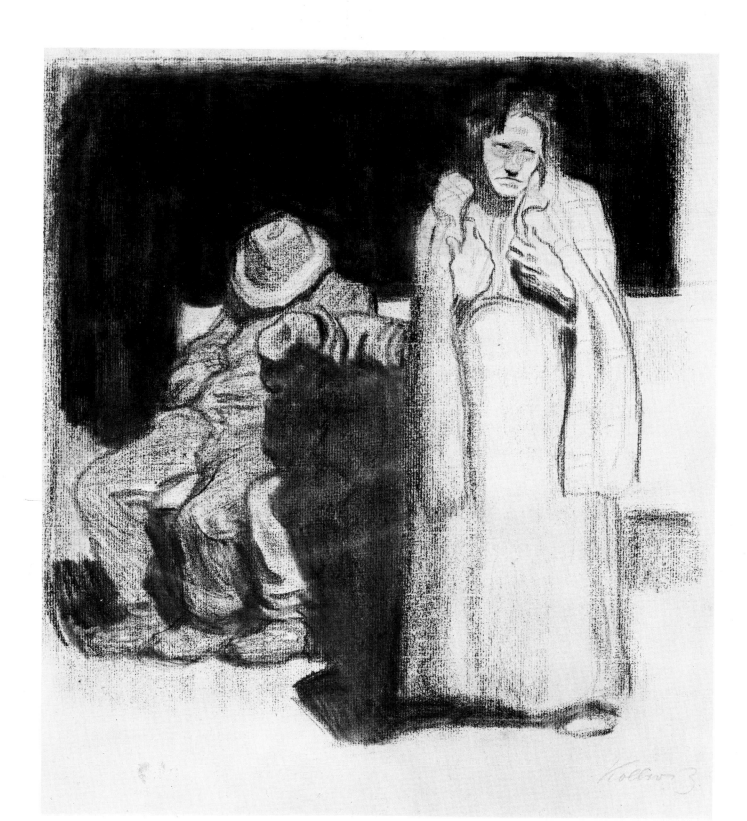

chapter 5
1909-1918

Last Years of Peace—
and the First World War

In 1909, Käthe Kollwitz began a series of drawings for *Simplicissimus*, a famous satirical magazine published in Munich. The editor entitled them *Pictures of Misery*. They show with power, pity, and love the anguish of the poor, the jobless, the homeless. Some critics believe that in her drawings, with their freedom and spontaneity of expression, the artist reached her highest levels, great as her graphic prints may be.

More and more, however, her work centered on mothers and children. Her art became a treasury of seemingly inexhaustible maternal love and concern. Death was sometimes an unwelcome intruder in these mother-child visions, as if a foretaste of the dark tragedy that was to strike her own life in 1914; or perhaps an after-echo of the death of her brother Benjamin.

In 1910 she made her first attempt at sculpture. Her drawings and graphic prints already had been approaching sculpture as she sought ever simpler, more massive, more decisive forms. With unfailing instinct she moved from two-dimensional drawing toward the creation of solid shapes, from linear precision to plastic power. Still, the incorruptible and tireless self-critic inside her rejected her first attempt at sculpture. She called it somewhat "dilettantish." Yet within about three decades she had become one of the finest sculptors of the first half of the twentieth century.

She was able to work more and more without models. This was largely the result of her growing mastery of the human form. Doing without models was also a great saving in time and money.

Though reserved and laconic with most people, she talked quite freely

"Homeless" (*Obdachlos*) Charcoal drawing, 1909. This drawing was intended for *Simplicissimus*, the satirical magazine published in Munich. *National Gallery of Art, Washington, D.C., Rosenwald Collection.*

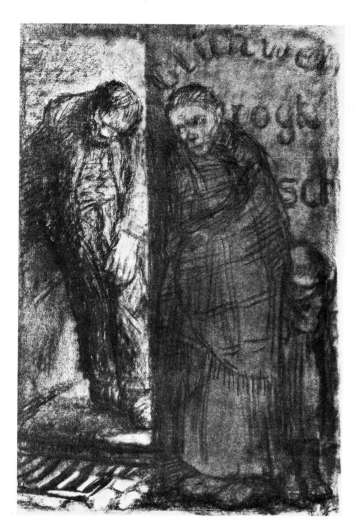 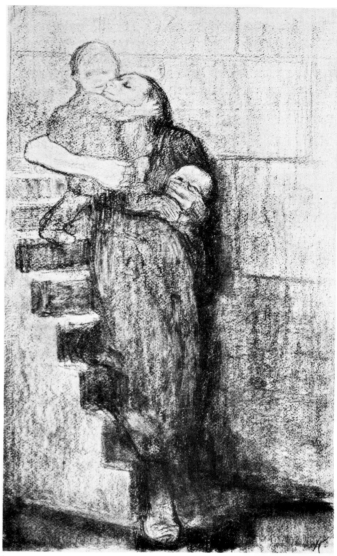

with models when she worked with them. Just as her art was her real way of communicating with the world, so the release she felt during the actual labor of creating it seemed to unlock even her oral communication, and she was able to talk more easily with her models than she could in her everyday nonworking life.

Her diary mentions two models who sat for her while she worked on a sculpture group in the autumn of 1910. One was a young woman working to support a sick husband and wonderful in her way with children. The other was a small boy, who, delighted with the woman model's nakedness, frolicked like a young faun. Käthe Kollwitz finally had to replace him with a girl because of his restlessness and his abundance of lice.

This sculpture group had a theme which became ever more dominant in the artist's mind: mothers clutching small children to their bodies—passionately, protectively, desperately. Sometimes the child was alive, sometimes already dead. In dozens of drawings, prints, and statues this situation is explored and intensified. It reaches stunning power in several sculptures: the "Protecting Mother" of 1937; the magnificent "Pietà" (1937–1938); and finally the "Tower of Mothers" of 1938, where several mother figures unite in a group to protect their children.

In 1912 her art again offended the authorities, just as the *Weavers* cycle had displeased the kaiser. A poster of hers had pictured a pale, semi-starved, working-class child carrying a baby sister in front of a sign that reads, "Playing prohibited on the stairs and in the courtyard." The poster advertised a meeting to protest housing conditions in Berlin, where more than half a million lived in rooms shared by five or more people. Hundreds of thousands of children, the poster stated, had no place to play. But calling attention to outrages was in itself an outrage to those who would rather have forgotten such things. From on high came the command—and the poster was banned by the police.

In the same year of 1912 the artist drew "Coal Strike" in charcoal

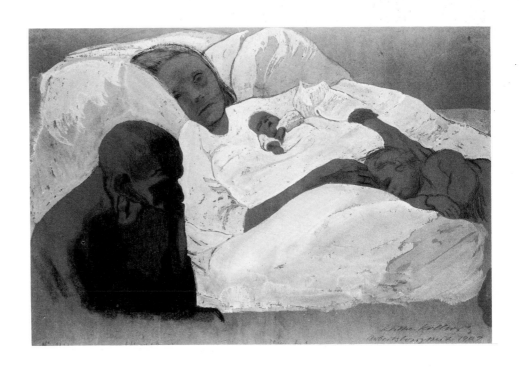

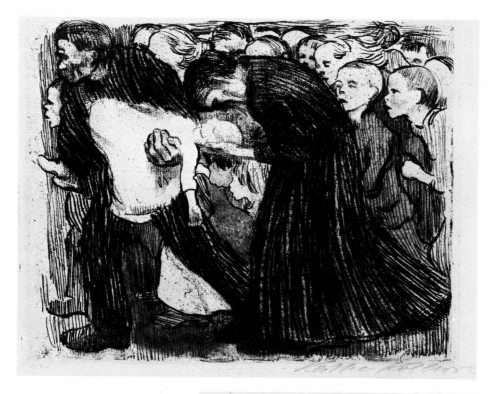

"Run Over" (*Überfahren*)
Soft-ground etching, 1910.

The dark richness possible with the soft-ground technique has been used here with striking emphasis. The size of the original is about 9¾ × 12½ inches.
Kunsthalle, Hamburg.

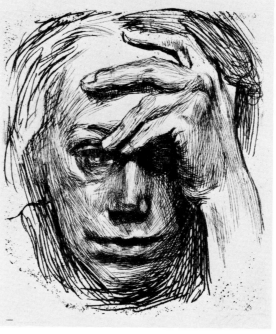

"Self-portrait with Hand on Forehead" (*Selbstbildnis mit der Hand an der Stirn*) Etching, 1910.

This memorable self-study has been called "incomplete"; however, it is one of the artist's most popular self-portraits.

The size of the original is only about 5⅞ × 5½ inches.

The original copper plate, while in its second state, was coated with steel to permit more prints to be made from it without too much deterioration. This is a print made from that "steeled" copper plate.
Deutsche Fotothek Dresden.

touched with white. It was exhibited later with this description: "A group of several workers in the foreground threatens with clenched fists two helmeted policemen. More strikers in the background." This is one of not more than two or three pictures in which the artist ever showed direct confrontation with police or armed authority.

Most of Käthe Kollwitz's works and interests suggest a very serious, possibly joyless, person. Yet her family and close friends knew her as one who craved fun and laughter and had a great capacity for both. As a young woman she had loved balls and sometimes would dance passionately and silently for hours. Her relative silence in social groups was perhaps due in part to a slight speech defect—a light lisp.

A writer who met her in 1912 wrote that more significant than the matter of spoken words, many or few, was the revelation made by "that place of suffering—her pale, broad-boned face." He called it the face of a seeress or

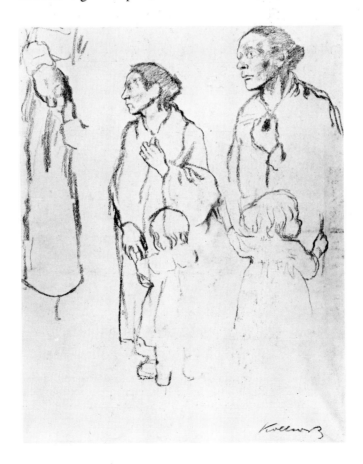

"Three Studies of a Woman with a Child" Drawing, undated. *Kunsthalle, Hamburg.*

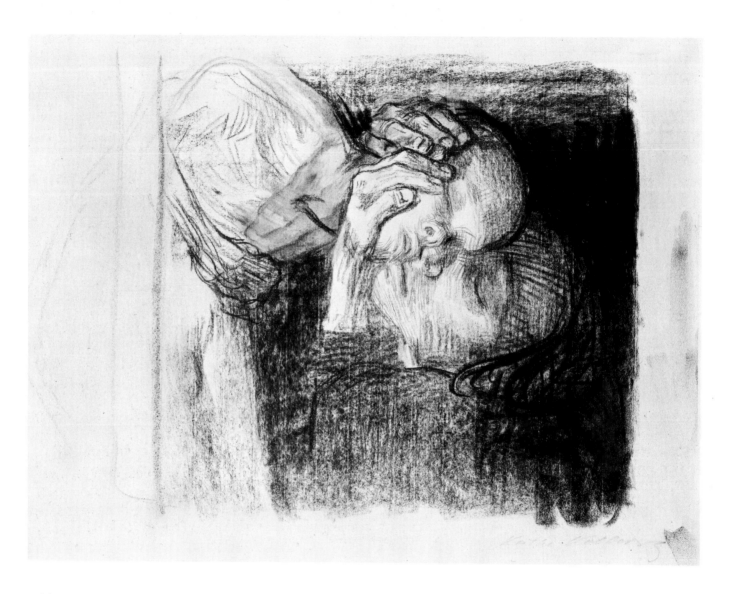

sybil and mentioned especially her eyes, "frighteningly knowing, yet gentle." By this time her hair showed much gray, and she was described as "prematurely old."

Occasionally she longed intensely to be free from domestic ties so as to go to Paris and concentrate on her sculpture. Nevertheless she felt also the need to be needed by her husband and sons. "When that ceases to be the case," she once wrote to Jeep, "I am afraid one enters a kind of Ice Age."

Beneath Imperial Germany's growing wealth, armaments, and expansionist

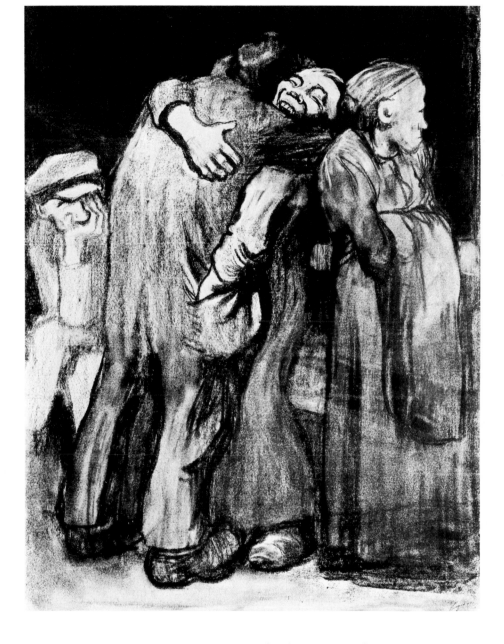

LEFT:
"Death, Mother, and Child"
(*Tod, Mutter und Kind*)
Charcoal drawing, 1910.

To the left of the mother's hands can be seen the not fully obliterated trace of another hand, which the artist had first drawn—then decided to move.
National Gallery of Art, Washington, D.C., Rosenwald Collection.

RIGHT:
"Dive" or "Flophouse"
(*Nachtasyl* or *Milieu*) Crayon drawing, about 1913 or 1914.
Deutsche Fotothek Dresden.

aims were deep-rooted social ills, never far from the surface. Käthe Kollwitz had been exposing many of them in her works during the past sixteen or seventeen years. Now, despite the blatant tub-thumping of the kaiser and other superpatriots, there were a few other eyes to see and voices to speak of these ills. It was in 1912 that Walter Rathenau, a wealthy industrialist (later to become foreign minister of postwar Germany), wrote: "Wherever I turn I see shadows arise. I see them evenings when I walk through the sordid streets of Berlin; when I see the insolence of our wealth grown mad;

when I perceive the hollowness of pompous words and hear tell of pseudo-Germanic exclusiveness. . . . An era is not free from care because army lieutenants feel joyful, or because the attachés of the foreign service are full of high expectations. For decades past, Germany has lived through no more ominous a period than this one."

But the reactionary men of wealth, finance, industry, civil service, and the military in Germany were drunk with nationalistic enthusiasm. They believed the pledges of their histrionic Kaiser Wilhelm II that he would lead them onward to still more splendid days and nights.

The shadows and sicknesses that Rathenau sensed and that Käthe Kollwitz had pointed to in some of her art works were similar—except for the accidents of language and superficial culture—to those that lurked under the glittering surface of such great cities as Paris, London, and St. Petersburg. In but a short time—within a couple of years in fact—the shams and deceptions of Germany and the rest of the West were to be exposed in an international conflict bloodier and more destructive than anything in the previous history of the world.

In 1912, however, the exchange of ideas, art, and culture still went on across national boundaries. In that year the first United States exhibition of the works of Käthe Kollwitz was held in New York.

The elder son, Hans, now nearly twenty, had begun the study of medicine in response to his father's advice and urging. His own hopes and enthusiasms had been entirely toward drama and the stage. Nothing else really attracted him. But he acquiesced finally and began the long, difficult path toward the degree of Doctor of Medicine. Meanwhile, the younger son, Peter, was showing signs of distinct ability as an artist.

Late 1912 found the forty-five-year-old Käthe Kollwitz discontented with her work and with herself. Almost all her available time that year had been given to sculpture. She had also worked on it during much of the previous year, but was dissatisfied with her progress. She wondered whether she would ever go back to etching. From then on, in fact, she seldom etched but concentrated rather on lithography and drawing, and also again and again on sculpture. Still later in 1919 she took up woodcutting. It was as if by 1912 she and etching had given each other the maximum possible, and she had to move ahead in other directions.

The first major descriptive catalogue of her graphic works, compiled by Johannes Sievers, appeared in 1913. She had published by that time about 120 different etchings and lithographs. A French edition of the Sievers catalogue was planned and had even been set in type when printing was halted in 1914 by the outbreak of the First World War.

The Kollwitzes, visiting in Königsberg during early August, heard the newly mobilized German soldiers singing as they marched by under the hotel room window. Käthe Kollwitz sat on the bed and "cried, and cried, and cried." From the first she knew what was to come.

Soon afterward, her younger son, Peter, now aged eighteen and filled with jingoistic patriotism, volunteered for the army. He was killed almost immediately, the first of his regiment on the night of October 22, 1914, near Diksmuide, Belgium. Käthe Kollwitz never fully recovered from the blow.

By the end of 1914 she began planning a sculptured memorial for her dead son. At first she attempted studies showing Peter's body stretched out horizontally with a mother figure standing at his feet and a father figure at his head. Somehow she could not complete this design. Constantly she brooded on the problem. Finally she decided that the memorial must be for *all* the war dead, the swiftly growing multitude of lost youth. She would portray *only* the mourning parents, representing all bereaved parents everywhere. However, it was not until 1924, ten years after Peter's death and six years after the First World War finally ended, that she was able to begin actual work on the "Mourning Parents."

To get at France more effectively the German army invaded Belgium, whose neutrality had been guaranteed by Germany as well as by the other major European powers. Following this breach of Belgian neutrality harsh and often brutal measures were used against resisting Belgians. The destruction wrought in the ancient city of Louvain was especially shocking. A world-wide protest followed. German leaders sought to answer or silence these reactions. In October of 1914 a manifesto was issued signed by nearly 200 German intellectuals. They included the dramatists Gerhart Hauptmann and Hermann Sudermann (1857–1928), the physicist Konrad Roentgen (1845–1923), and scores of others—scholars, professors, historians, and artists.

All set their names to the ridiculous and even pitiful assertion that German culture was a civilizing force in the world and that there was no German wrongdoing in this war. Indeed, "It is not true that we have criminally violated the neutrality of Belgium [or] . . . that our troops have brutally destroyed Louvain."

The name of Käthe Kollwitz was not signed to this roster. Her attitude may at first have been hesitant or even bewildered, but she assuredly did not join the rush of warmongers.

From 1915 onward a phrase began to appear in her diary and letters: "Seed for the planting shall not be ground up!" She was making clear the need to save the youth of the land from the war. Peter had been such seed for the future. She had carried and nurtured that seed. Gladly she and her husband would have died instead, if Peter, their seed, could have lived! The phrase came from a letter in the novel *Wilhelm Meister* by her beloved Goethe. This thought—that seed set aside to be sown must not be destroyed—was to be expressed by Käthe Kollwitz more than once during the two monstrous world wars that were fought during her lifetime.

Again and again her diary and letters voiced grief and longing for Peter. She tried to probe the darkness, seeking meanings and answers. The young were going to war "willingly and gladly" in Germany and other nations also. Young people who would otherwise be friends were killing each other.

"Is youth really without judgment?" she asked. "Do they always march to the attack on command . . . ? Does youth really want war?" Or would only an "old youth" give up wanting it? Persuaded that war was senseless, she then asked herself, "What should be the law of life for men?" It could not be to attain the maximum of private personal happiness. Rather life must be placed in the service of an idea.

But Peter and the others *had* placed their lives in the service of the idea of love of the Fatherland. So too had the youth of England, Russia, and France. And with what result? ". . . the wild attack against each other, the impoverishment of all that is most beautiful in Europe."

Youth in all these countries had been betrayed, she concluded. How had this been possible? Was their dedication deliberately exploited in order to bring about the war? Who was responsible? "Where are the guilty ones?"

Youth was not alone. "Has everyone been deceived? Has there been a mass madness . . . ? And when and how will there be an awakening?" It was not enough to weep for the dead. One must be worthy of them. "We must work to make this the last war."

She labored slowly at her art. A plaster statue called "The Lovers," made in 1913, was exhibited at the Berlin Free Secession show of 1916. In

Three studies of a bearded worker. Drawing, undated. Probably from about 1913 to 1915.

There is a notation in the center to the effect that the hand (resting on the knee) is "too large."
Kunsthalle, Hamburg.

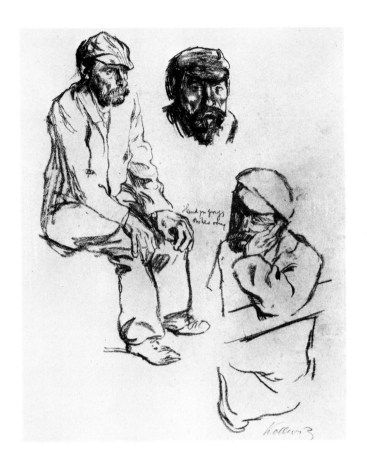

1916, too, she drew a mother whose dead son was slipping from her arms. It linked her past themes to future ones.

June thirteenth of that year brought her twenty-fifth wedding anniversary and Karl's fifty-third birthday. Her mother had told her as she was about to be married that Karl's love would never be found wanting. So it had proved. Her diary for that day contains a grateful and beautiful tribute to him.

Through her art she joined hands with a minority in Germany who tried to oppose the war madness. Paul Cassirer, an important art dealer and publisher, brought out an illustrated periodical entitled *Bildermann*, remarkably bold in its antiwar content. The issue of August 20, 1916, carried a Kollwitz lithograph of a happy, laughing mother and child. Below it a six-line verse told of poverty and food shortage, sharply contrasting with the joy in the picture.

In July 1917 her fiftieth birthday was commemorated with a retrospective showing of her works at the Cassirer Gallery, sponsored by the Berlin Secession group. This was a real honor. Some 150 of her drawings and prints, plus a few sculptures, were shown. A number of the pictures

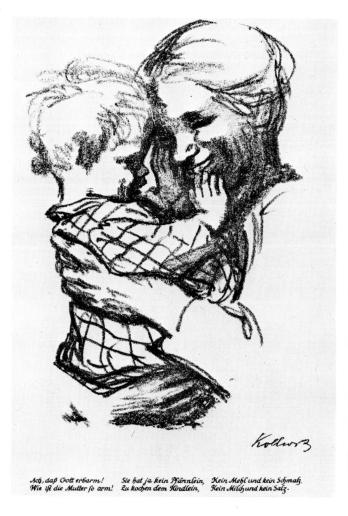

Ach, daß Gott erbarm! Sie hat ja kein Pfännlein, Kein Mehl und kein Schmalz,
Wie ist die Mutter so arm! Zu kochen dem Kindlein, Kein Milch und kein Salz.

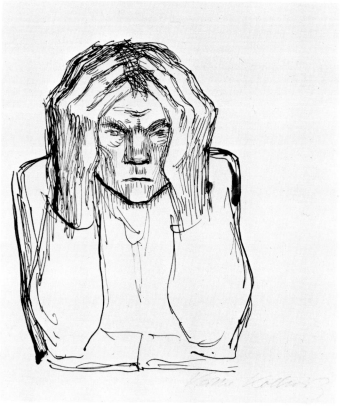

reflected indelibly the realities and tragedies of the war. Since the first success of her *Weavers* series, twenty years had passed. The socialist artist had come far and achieved much.

She herself felt that the show ". . . must mean something, for all these works are extracts of my life. . . . Never have I done a work cold . . . but always, so to speak, with my blood."

At the Cassirer Gallery in November 1917 she attended a showing of the works of another great German graphic artist and sculptor, Ernst Barlach (1870–1938). She was deeply moved. She felt an immediate need to return to her own studio to work, work, work . . .

Barlach, a man of many talents and some genius, was to have important effects on her in the future. She, in turn, was to be reflected in his work. Never an imitator, she was always a student, eager to learn with the help of others. Barlach above all now seemed to have much to offer.

Late in the First World War, as Germany was obviously losing, a well-known German poet, Richard Dehmel (1863–1920), issued an appeal urging even young boys and old men to rally to the Fatherland for a last resistance on the field of battle. Before the war Dehmel had been regarded as a crusader for social justice and progress. As such he had been looked up to by many young writers and artists.

Now a courageous reply by Käthe Kollwitz was published in two important newspapers, the *Vorwärts* of the Socialist Party and the respectable old *Vossische Zeitung* of Berlin. Her open letter ended with the burning words: "There has been enough of dying! Let not another man fall! Against Richard Dehmel I call upon one greater who said, 'Seed for the planting shall not be ground up!'"

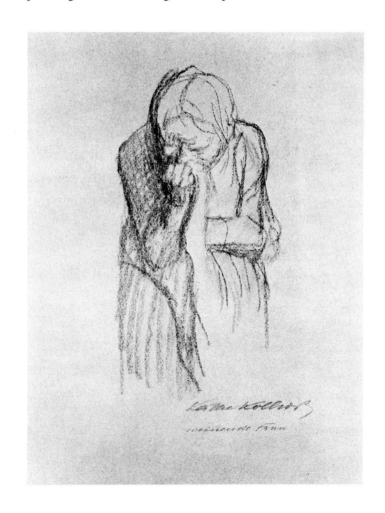

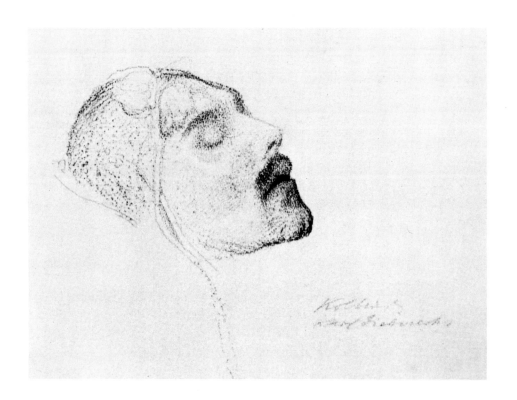

"Karl Liebknecht in Death"
(*Liebknecht auf dem
Totenbett*) Drawing, 1919.
Deutsche Fotothek Dresden.

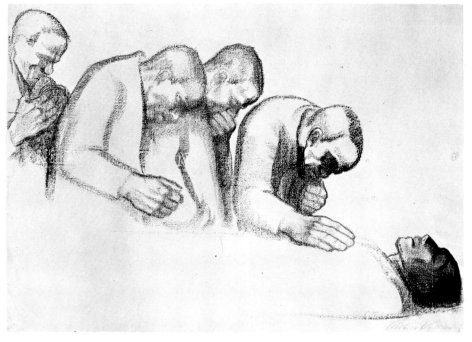

Another of the artist's many
studies for the Liebknecht
memorial picture. Lithographic
crayon, about 1920.

Here again, the artist worked
with the concept of a row of
four mourners above the prone
body of their lost leader, Karl
Liebknecht. The museum
name for it is "The Mourners."
*Santa Barbara Museum of Art.
Gift of Mrs. Dorothy Brown.*

chapter 6
1918-1924

"The War Is Over, but There Is No Peace"

November 1918 brought an end to the terrible First World War. Defeat led to a so-called revolution in Germany. The kaiser fled to the Netherlands, taking with him his artistic prejudices. But the old powers remained: big business and finance, the military hierarchy, East Prussian landowners, the reactionary establishments in courts, civil service, and education. Social Democratic leaders, aided by army units, police, and the judiciary, crushed the revolts by Spartacists and other left-wing groups. The new Weimar Republic got off to a bad start. Käthe Kollwitz in her diary and letters revealed her fears that the roots of reaction in Germany remained uncut. The war was over, but there was no real peace. Poverty was bitter, inflation was threatening.

Though greatly disturbed by postwar events, the artist was jubilant that the fighting was over. On December 8, 1918, she and her son, Hans, attended a freedom celebration in Berlin. Here she listened with some disapproval to a speech by a leading Social Democratic politician, then was uplifted by a performance of Beethoven's Ninth Symphony, climaxing in its choral "Ode to Joy." This, she wrote, represented socialism in its purest form.

Early in 1919, Käthe Kollwitz became the first woman elected to the Prussian Academy of Arts. Other new members included fifteen men, with Ernst Barlach among them. Later that year she received the coveted title of Professor, though she declared, "I am against all titles." Now she was allowed free use of a studio in the Academy building. Personnel records of the Academy show that in answer to the query regarding her religion she listed herself as a dissident, or nonconformist, rather than as one without religion.

The first years of the German Republic were marked by upheaval and change, much of which was reflected in her work. Emotionally and artistically committed she took a stand against the so-called *Fehme* murders —the assassinations of radical and liberal leaders by reactionary gangs. In mid-January 1919 members of the counterrevolutionary Free Corps brutally murdered an extraordinary man and woman, Karl Liebknecht and Rosa Luxemburg, founders of the young German Communist Party.

Käthe Kollwitz had not entirely agreed with Liebknecht politically, but she was horrified by his assassination. Later she read his letters and was brought even closer to him. She sketched his body as it lay in the morgue and was deeply stirred by the grief shown by hundreds of thousands of people at his grave and the graves of thirty-eight others also murdered during this bloody period of reaction. Liebknecht alone among the hundreds of deputies in the Reichstag had refused to approve funds for the war while it was going on. His record in that and many other things had been a brilliant one.

During the next two years she worked and reworked her sketches of the dead Liebknecht. They became first an etching, then a lithograph, and finally a stark, powerful woodcut. The sequence was significant of her own rapid development at that bitter time.

She had been working on a poster memorial for Liebknecht when, in June 1920, she visited the Berlin Secession exhibition and saw woodcuts by Ernst Barlach. "They completely bowled me over." She now looked at her own lithographs with dissatisfaction. "Barlach has found his way," she told her diary, "and I have not yet found mine."

Yet just over eight months before, she had decided that for her lithography had become the only possible technique, because it was ". . . so simple . . . hardly a technique at all."

Stimulated by Barlach, she worked more and more on woodcuts. She had completed her first woodcut, "Two Dead," in 1919. In 1920 she finished her "Memorial for Karl Liebknecht." By 1929 she had created more than forty woodcuts—a medium anything but simple, making difficult demands on the artist and indeed also on the viewer.

The artistic lives of Kollwitz and Barlach ran parallel in several ways. Each respected and admired the other. Yet both were reserved, and they had

"Memorial for Karl Liebknecht" (*Gedenkblatt für Karl Liebknecht*) Woodcut, started 1919, completed 1920. The size of the original is about 13⅝ × 19½ inches.

The final form—stark, tragic, austere, and yet incandescent. In this last state, she added the words at bottom: *Die Lebenden dem Toten. Erinnerung an den 15. Januar 1919.* (The Living to the Dead. In Memory of the 15th January, 1919.) This title is a reversal of the title of a great poem by Freiligrath that the artist had loved as a girl: *Die Toten an die Lebenden* (From the Dead to the Living).

In place of the four mourners of her earlier studies, the artist here shows no less than fifteen figures, including a mother and infant, whose stricken faces tell what Liebknecht had meant to their hopes for the future. The strange, straight, abstracted form of the dead man's body represents a treatment that Kollwitz used more than once. The body has become, by a strange transformation, like a fallen pillar or the shaft of a horizontal monument. *Fogg Art Museum, Harvard University.*

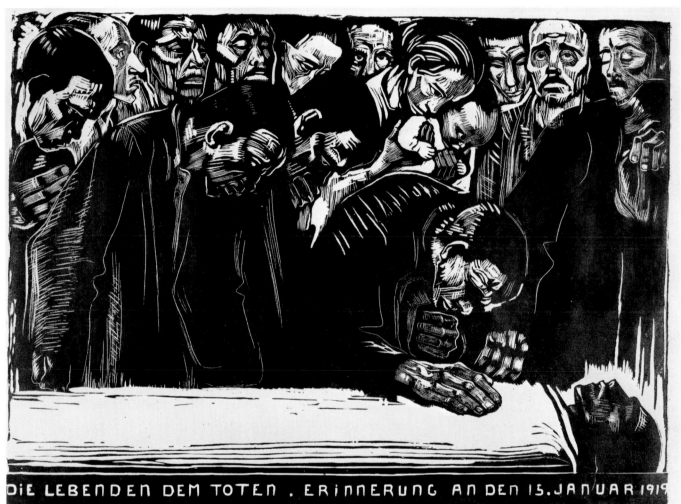

DIE LEBENDEN DEM TOTEN . ERINNERUNG AN DEN 15. JANUAR 1919

little personal contact. Each in an individual and enduring manner created an anticlassical concept of beauty; each, accustomed to expression through art, spoke out against social injustice, militarism, and war.

The years following World War I brought much reason for protest. Hunger and malnutrition ravaged millions of Germans. To meet emergencies, the government began to print more and more money. Inflation increased, finally wiping out all savings and many investments. As the value of money melted away, so too did moral standards. Germany was likened at this time to an enormous insane asylum.

73

In her diary for October 23, 1923, the artist noted that now one American dollar was worth 40 *billion* German marks! A general strike was threatened. "Hunger and helplessness are everywhere," she wrote. "My spirits are heavy and depressed."

There was no need now to turn to history for compelling drama. She was caught up in the horrors of her own time: the death and destruction of the wartime period; the hunger, degradation, and injustice of the present. She responded with many unforgettable pictures. Some, resembling transfigured posters, summoned people to action against future wars and warmakers. She found that inflation interfered with her modest needs in art. Lithographic stones were enormously expensive, hard to find and get delivered. But she worked on.

In 1920 she joined the International Workers Aid (IAH), a left-oriented organization for relief. Its sponsors included other eminent artists and thinkers such as Albert Einstein, Georg Grosz, Maxim Gorki, Anatole France, Henri Barbusse, and Upton Sinclair.

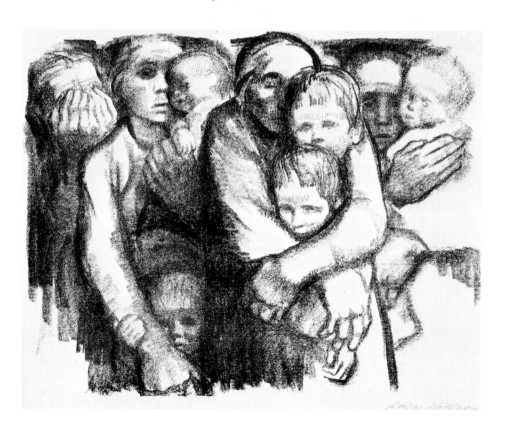

"Mothers" (*Mütter*) Lithograph, 1919.
One of many enduring interpretations of the abandoned victims of all wars: the widows and orphans. It is actually a second version of the subject; the first was an etching. The artist, apparently, after attempting alterations with the aquatint process, felt dissatisfied and discarded the etching—replacing it with this triumphant lithograph. *Kunsthalle, Hamburg.*

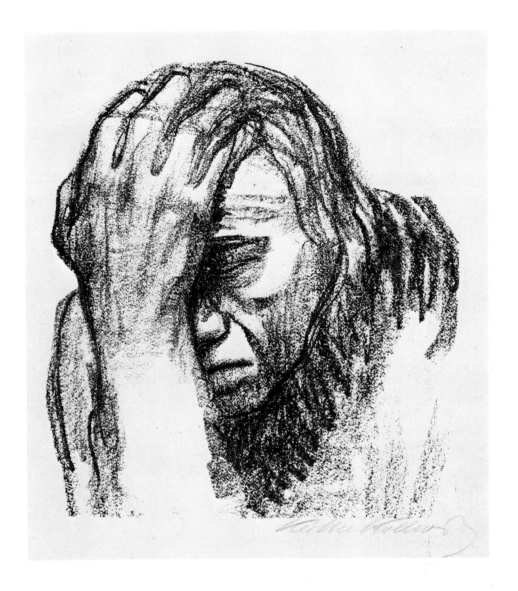

"Woman Thinking"
(*Nachdenkende Frau*)
Lithograph, 1920. The size of
the original drawing on the
lithographic stone is about
11½ × 10½ inches.
Kunsthalle, Hamburg.

"Help Russia" and "Vienna is Dying! Save her Children!" were two of the powerful lithographed posters she created to meet immediate needs. As she sketched the starving children of Vienna, scourged by the whip of a giant Death, she wept along with the figures she drew.

"I feel the burden . . ." she wrote. "I must not draw back from the task of acting as an advocate. I must speak out about the sufferings of the people." That suffering did not seem to end; rather, it ". . . towers as high as a mountain."

Her poster "Help Russia" was carried all over Germany, especially by the gifted writer Theodore Plivier (1892–1955), to collect funds for the relief of the famine in Russia. The artist made two portraits of Plivier in 1923 before his books became successful.

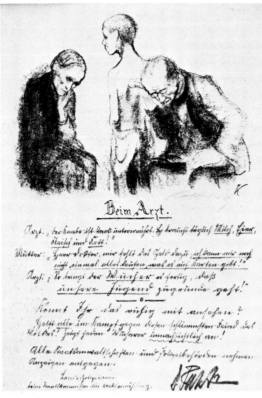

"At the Doctor's" (*Beim Arzt*) Lithograph, 1920.

This is the third of the three posters against usury. The text begins with a dialogue between the doctor and the mother. He recommends that the boy should be fed milk and other nourishing foods daily. The mother, however, cannot afford it. The doctor replies with a denunciation of usury and its effect on German children.

The size of the orginal lithographic image is about 7½ × 10 inches.
Deutsche Fotothek Dresden.

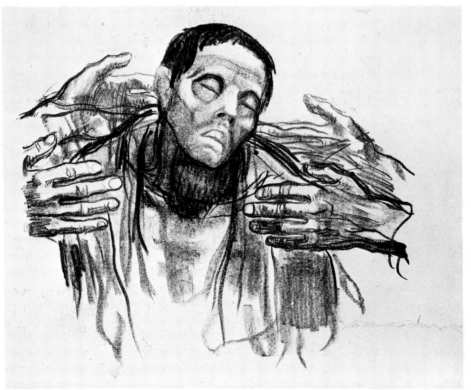

"Help Russia" (*Helft Russland*) Lithograph, 1921.

In the first state, this print included the bold appeal, "Help/ Russia" and below, the address of the committee conducting the drive for funds.
Kunsthalle, Hamburg.

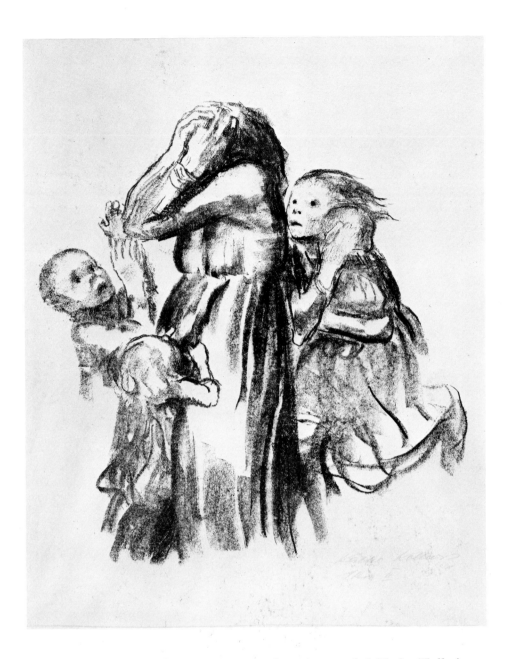

"Fallen" (*Gefallen*) Lithograph, 1921. The title is sometimes given as "Killed in Action." *Kunsthalle, Hamburg.*

The socialists of Germany more and more regarded Käthe Kollwitz as the illustrator of their aims and ideals. In 1920 *Rote Fahne*, the official German Communist newspaper, carried an article about her. Her work, it stated, could be divided into two periods—the earlier, revolutionary (referring especially to the *Weavers* and *Peasants' War* series), and the later, showing the working class only in oppressed and hopeless situations. The latter, in the opinion of the article, was deplorable rather than praiseworthy.

The artist did not agree. She saw no such sharp division in her work. She did grant, however, that she no longer advocated revolution—not in the

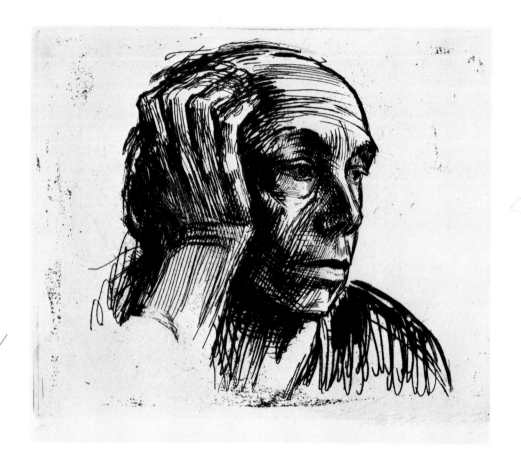

"Self-portrait" (*Selbstbildnis*)
Etching, 1921.
Kunsthalle, Hamburg.

sense of hate, violence, or retaliation. She had seen too much of the revolution that had followed the recent World War.

In creating the dynamic "Outbreak" print for her *Peasants' War* series in 1903, she felt she had reached the summit of what she had to offer the revolutionary movement. Now she would have turned entirely from the political and dealt only with general human situations but for the events of the postwar struggles: the brutal murders of Liebknecht, Luxemburg, and the others; the impoverishment and the hunger. All this led her to portray these evils with passion and sorrow in the effort to remedy them.

"They should have left me quietly alone," she told her diary in a momentary weakening of her feminism. ". . . an artist, and a woman at that," couldn't be expected ". . . to find her way about in this insane, complex state of affairs."

As an artist she felt entitled ". . . to draw out of myself the content of

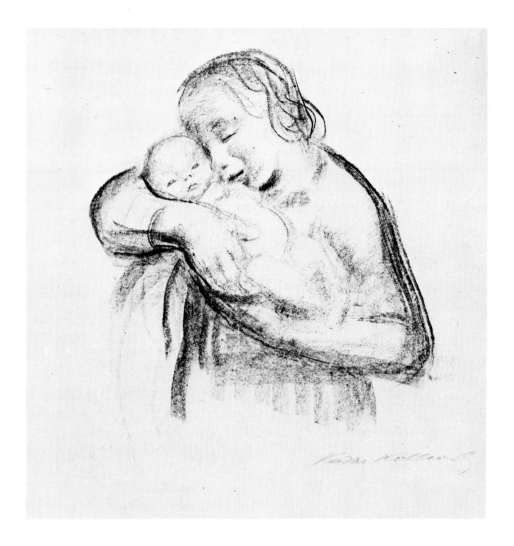

"Mother with Infant" Crayon sketch, undated, but quite possibly from the 1922–1923 period.

The evidence suggests that this was a study preliminary to the making of the woodcut, "The Sacrifice" (*Das Opfer*). The size of the original drawing is about 14⅜ × 13⅝ inches. *Staatliche Museen zu Berlin.*

my feelings, to let it work on me, to portray it." That same right justified her also in showing the working class saying good-bye to Liebknecht, and even in dedicating that portrayal to the workers—without herself having to follow Liebknecht politically. But then, significantly, she revealed her uncertainty by adding a question which meant, "Or do I *not* have this right?"

She and her husband attended a revival of Hauptmann's drama *The Weavers*, now more than twenty-eight years past its first historic performance. Again she felt the surge of feeling that had swept her so long before. She searched herself. Just where did she stand politically?

She was only an evolutionary she concluded in her diary, not a revolutionary. And she asked herself: Was she even more of a democrat than a socialist? Revolution, in reality, was not the ideal thing some writers suggested. Its true face had to be earthy, dirty—not ideal. It was not the face she had seen in her girlhood dreams of manning the barricades.

79

This dialogue between her mind and emotions never completely ended. Its tensions supplied her work with much of its power and poignancy. Even as she told herself she could no longer be a revolutionary, her work did not abandon the struggle or lose its strength.

Soon after the war her son, Hans, now a doctor like his father, married an artist named Ottilie Ehlers. Their first son was born in 1921 and named Peter for the boy killed in 1914. Käthe Kollwitz became a joyful grandmother. She loved to visit the baby Peter and his parents, who lived in Lichtenrade, a southern suburb of Berlin. Three more grandchildren were born: twin girls, Jutta and Jördis, and another boy, Arne-Andreas Kollwitz.

The need to continue work dominated the life of Käthe Kollwitz despite all personal attachments. She compared her own cycles of creativity with the experiences of other artists, especially the writer Hermann Hesse (1877–1962), who lamented the sequences of ups and downs in his work. She could not find that for her there was any predictable rhythm. Rather she thought that she had just a certain flow or supply of inner energy to give. At times she made full use of this, then later she had to be content with less, until her inner reservoirs were filled once again.

She had still to speak her feelings in pictures about the horrors of war from the viewpoint of woman as wife and mother. In 1920 she began a *War* series, first as etchings, then as lithographs. Finally, dissatisfied with these attempts, she redid them as seven stark, tense, shattering woodcuts, with the titles "The Sacrifice," "The Volunteers," "The Parents," "The Widow" (two treatments), "The Mothers," and "The People."

A full year of intense work went into the seven wood blocks. Some, like "The Parents," she did over and over. Her self-criticism never lapsed. First she found the print too light, too hard, too clear. It had to be changed—for she noted that ". . . pain is very dark." Beyond doubt, she did succeed in portraying the darkness of pain.

More than once she returned to the theme of the woodcut "The Mothers." In 1930 she was commissioned to adapt it, much enlarged, for a community house in Saarbrücken to the west. And as late as 1937 she resumed the theme in her fine bronze sculpture called "Tower of Mothers."

The artist wrote on October 23, 1922, regarding the *War* woodcut series to the eminent French novelist and critic Romain Rolland (1866–1944), expressing her intention to have these prints travel throughout the world to tell everyone in a complete, conclusive way, "This is how it was—this is what we have all borne during these unspeakably bad years." That world-wide

"The Parents" (*Die Eltern*)
Woodcut, 1923. Third print
in the seven-print series *War*
(*Krieg*). The size of the
original woodblock, which is
lost, was about 13¾ × 16⅜
inches.
Kunsthalle, Hamburg.

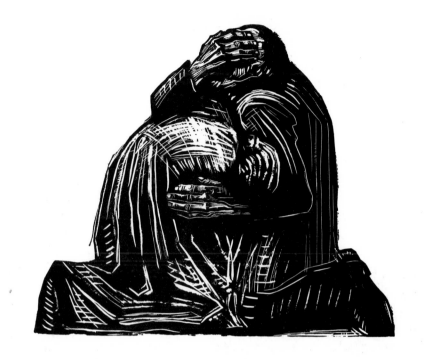

"The Volunteers" (*Die
Freiwilligen*) Woodcut,
1922–1923. The second print
in the series *War* (*Krieg*).

   Death is the mad, forward-
striding drummer, followed by
the young men who have
volunteered to fight. The
two farthest right are still
shouting patriotic slogans.
Ahead of them is the tortured
face (eyes hidden) of one who
has just been wounded. Ahead
of him, center, is the
unconscious form of one dying.
And farthest left, is a glassy-
eyed soldier, presumably already
dead.
Kunsthalle, Hamburg.

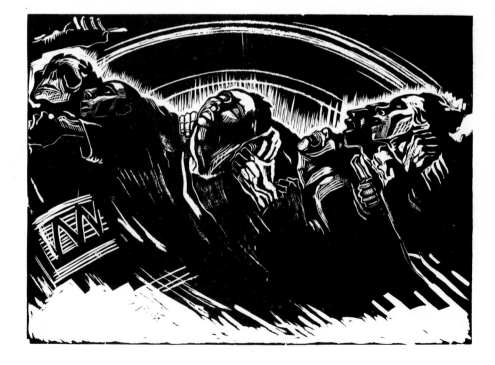

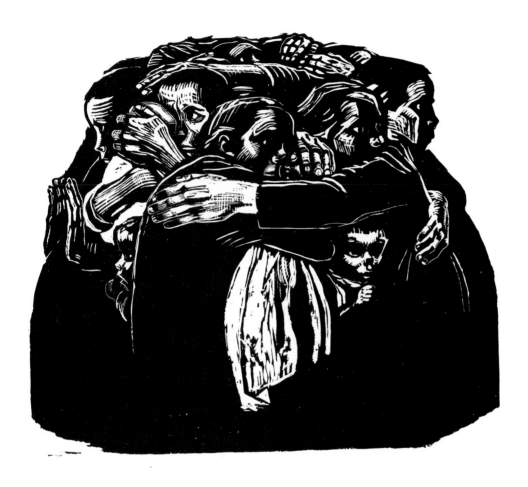

journey began in 1924 when the prints were published in portfolio form. It has not yet ended.

Early in the 1920s Kollwitz made a memorable statement of purpose in her diary. She had attended a memorial meeting for the war dead and now wrote of her "warm, gratifying feeling" because she knew herself to be part of an international group working against war. She freely admitted that her art was not *pure*, in the sense of art for art's sake. But it was art nonetheless.

"Everyone must work as he can. I agree that my art has purpose." And that purpose was ". . . to be effective in this time when people are so helpless and in need of aid." On this she felt no confusion or doubt. "My way is clear and evident."

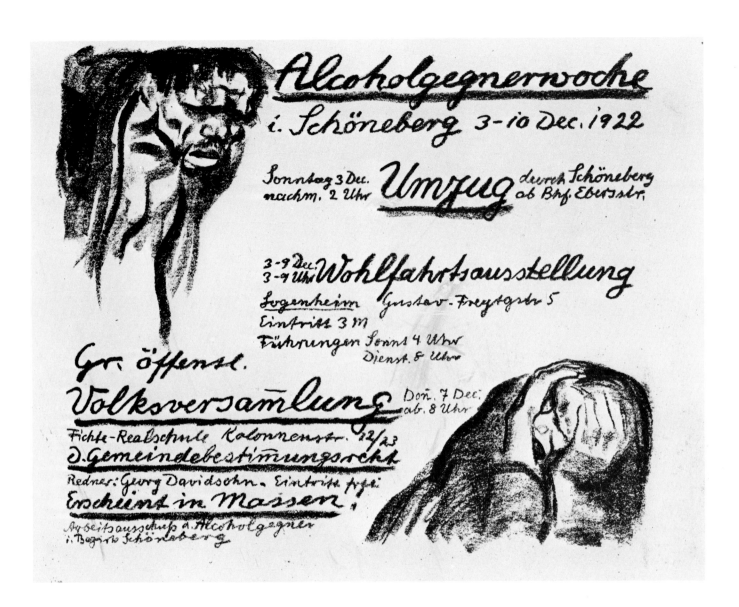

Poster for the Anti-alcohol
Week (*Alcoholgegnerwoche*)
Lithograph, 1922. The size of
the orginal lithographic stone,
now lost, was about 13¼ × 15⅝
inches.

The artist executed the entire
poster, including the lettering,
for an anti-alcoholism drive.
The poster urges participation
in a parade and attendance at an
exhibition and mass meeting.
Staatliche Museen zu Berlin.

When asked to do an antiwar poster for the International Trade Union
Federation, she told her friend the painter Erna Kruger of her joy at the
opportunity. "One can say a thousand times that it is not pure art [because]
it includes a purpose, [but] I want to be effective with my art as long as I
can." The outcome, entitled "The Survivors," was a lithographed poster for
the Antiwar Day of September 21, 1924. It carried the slogan "War against
War."

Käthe Kollwitz's posters must be included among her most powerful
compositions. Besides those mentioned, she made "Germany's Children Are
Hungry!" and "Bread!" both in 1924; and that fierce, silent cry of determination, "Never Again War!" for a Youth Day held in August 1924 at Leipzig.

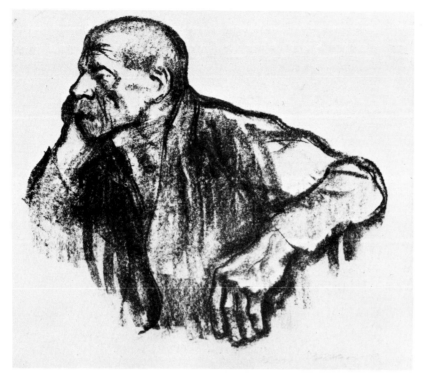

"Seated Worker" (*Sitzender Arbeiter*) Lithograph, 1923. The stone, now destroyed, was about 12⅞×14 inches.

Originally, this lithograph was meant to be used on a portfolio of works issued in honor of the sixtieth birthday of an artist, Arno Holz, but subsequently another lithograph by Kollwitz was chosen.
Deutsche Fotothek Dresden.

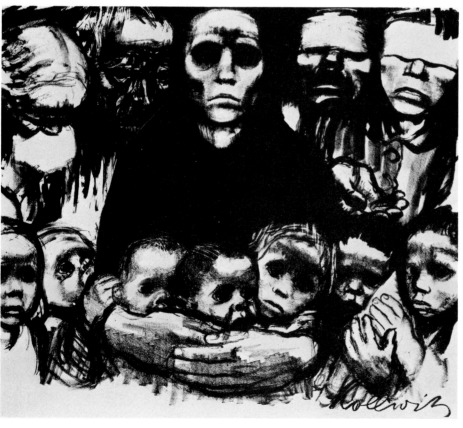

"The Survivors" (*Die Überlebenden*) Lithograph, 1923. The original lithographic stone was destroyed. The size of this image on it was about 22⅛ × 27 inches.

This is a print from the first state, before the text for the poster was added. At the lower right appeared the slogan "War Against War!" and in the center the announcement of the Antiwar Day, September 21, 1924.
Kunsthalle, Hamburg.

"Germany's Children Are Hungry!" (*Deutschlands Kinder Hungern!*) Lithograph, 1924.

This picture was made for a poster which the artist completed by writing the title to the right. The poster was about 17 × 27 inches. This popular picture came to be used again and again for all sorts of causes and fund collections, some of which failed to credit the artist by name.
Kunsthalle, Hamburg.

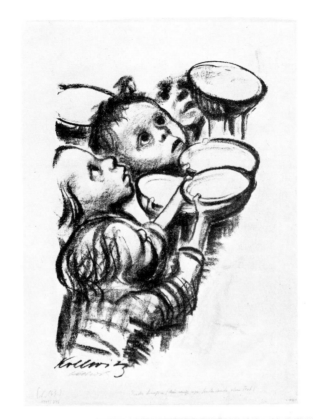

"Bread!" (*Brot!*) Lithograph, 1924.

The original stone has been destroyed, but this picture has been reproduced repeatedly by means of photolithographic processes. It is possibly one of the three or four most widely distributed works of the artist.
Staatliche Museen zu Berlin.

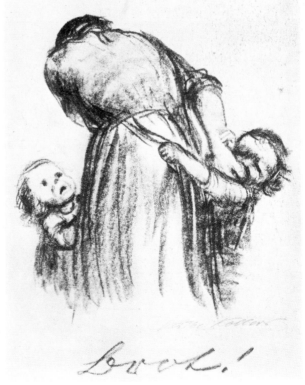

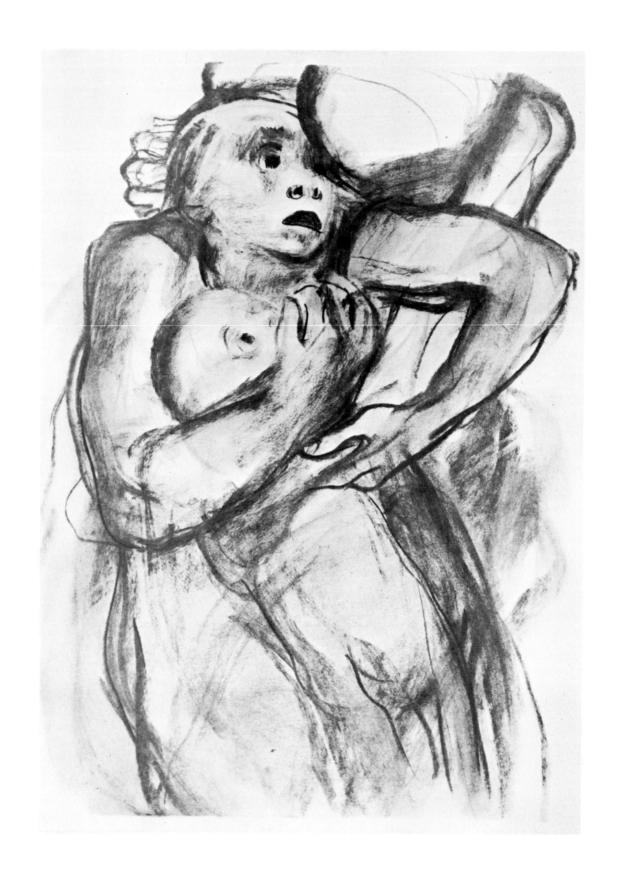

LEFT:
"Death Seizes a Woman"
Charcoal drawing, 1923–1924.
  One of the eight drawings
in the series *Parting
and Death* (*Abschied und
Tod*). This was a study for a
similar lithograph, completed
in 1934—some ten years later
—as the fourth in the eight-print
series called *Death* (*Tod*).
Deutsche Fotothek Dresden.

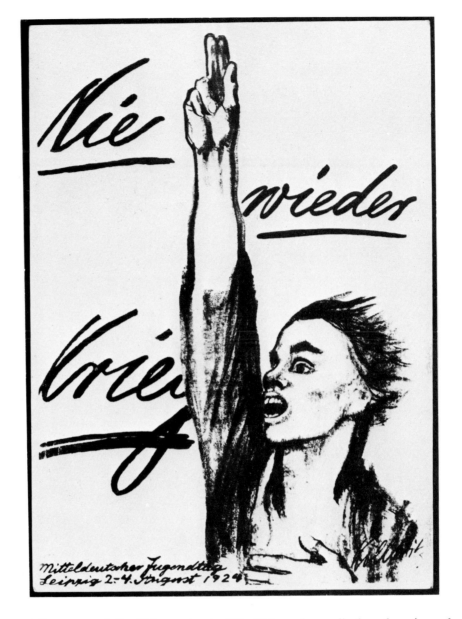

RIGHT:
"Never Again War!" Litho-
graph poster, 1924. The words
at bottom left mean: The
Central Germany Youth Day,
Leipzig, August 2–4, 1924.
Deutsche Fotothek Dresden.

These, especially "Never Again War!" have been displayed again and again,
often without credit to the artist. The young man with upraised arm and two
fingers extended is taking a solemn oath in the German manner. That symbolic oath was to seem a bitter mockery within a few years.

  Death, which had haunted her life, now began more and more to appear
as a symbolic figure in her art. In 1923 and 1924 she worked on a series of
eight drawings called *Parting and Death*. The beauty and power of her
draftsmanship in these drawings foreshadow the grim, gripping series of
eight lithographs called simply *Death*, completed in 1934 and 1935, during
the early years of the death-dealing Nazi regime.

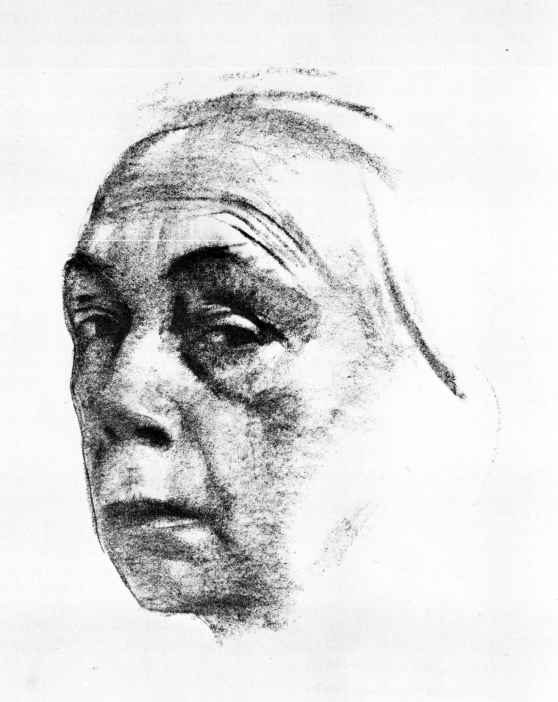

chapter 7
1924-1932

One Mourning Mother
Speaks for Many

The First World War—which had been hailed by some as a war to end war —was over by some six years. It was ten years since the artist's younger son, Peter, had been killed in 1914. Still she struggled unsuccessfully to provide for him and the other war dead a memorial that she considered worthy. From time to time she would unwrap her incomplete attempts at the sculpture in clay; then, dissatisfied and depressed, she would cover them over again, still incomplete.

One day came word that Peter's body was to be moved from its separate grave to a collective and official soldiers' cemetery at Roggevelde, Essen, near the small town of Diksmuide, Belgium. This news spurred her purposes and dispelled her doubts. In the summer of 1926 she traveled to Belgium and studied intently the site of the new cemetery and its environment. Once back in Berlin she began work again on the memorial. Yet nearly five years of labor passed before she finally completed plaster models of the figures, and it was 1932 before they were finished in enduring stone.

During this period she created many other works. In 1932 she finished *Proletariat*, a series of three dark, forbidding, yet powerfully fascinating woodcuts, individually called "Unemployed," "Children's Death," and "Hunger." They had been reworked again and again. Fifteen different versions, or states, are known for "Hunger" alone.

The beginning of 1925 had brought the death of her mother at the age of eighty-seven. Frau Katharina Schmidt had been living with Käthe and

"Self-portrait" (*Selbstbildnis*) Lithograph, 1924.
This print ranks with some of the greatest self-portraits in art history. The image on the lithographic stone, which has been destroyed, was about 11¼ × 9 inches.
Fogg Art Museum, Harvard University.

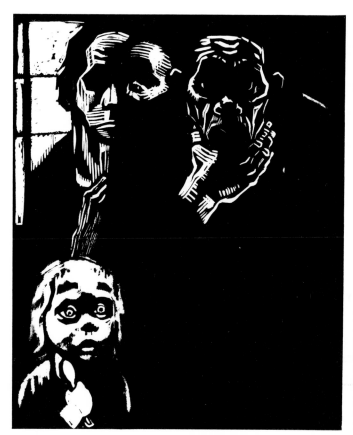

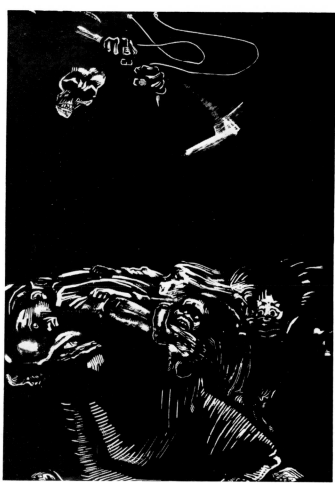

Karl Kollwitz, and although she had become mentally confused, her loss was a blow to them both.

Nearing the end of her fifty-eighth year the artist evaluated her situation. She noted three things that meant the most to her in life: she had had children; she had a faithful companion, her husband; and she had her work.

Her diaries repeatedly praise Karl as her "life's comrade." She did not gloss over differences or difficulties their marriage brought, but she found he had grown and developed without losing what she called "an innocent heart" and an inner gladness. The passing years brought them even closer. Kollwitz noted once that her diaries devoted most space to her sorrows, depressions, and troubles and did not sufficiently reflect the happy times, which she seems to have felt less need to record.

In 1926 a large exhibition of her work was held in New York City for the purpose of raising money to aid German children. She herself, despite her fame, earned but little from art. Her earnings came to only a couple of thousand marks a year—roughly $500. Realistically she called this ridiculously

ABOVE LEFT:
"Jobless" or "Unemployed" (*Erwerbslos*) Woodcut, 1925. First print from the series *Proletariat*, a three-print cycle, all woodcuts. *Kupferstichkabinett, Dresden. Photograph taken by Deutsche Fotothek Dresden.*

ABOVE RIGHT:
"Hunger" Woodcut, 1925. Second print from the *Proletariat* woodcut series.
One of the most reworked of the Kollwitz graphics. No less than fifteen different states of this block are recorded, of which this is probably an example of the final state. *Deutsche Fotothek Dresden.*

RIGHT:
"Visit to the Children's Hospital" (*Besuch im Kinderkrankenhaus*) Lithograph, 1926.
Deutsche Fotothek Dresden.

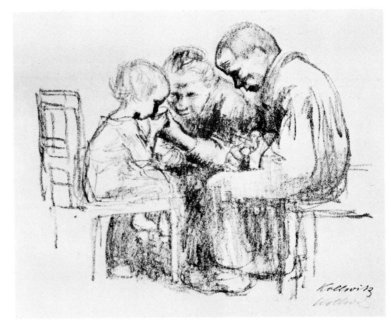

"Municipal Shelter" (*Städtisches Obdach*) Lithograph, 1926.
 This is also known as "Homeless." It was made first as a drawing for the Salvation Army.
Fogg Art Museum, Harvard University.

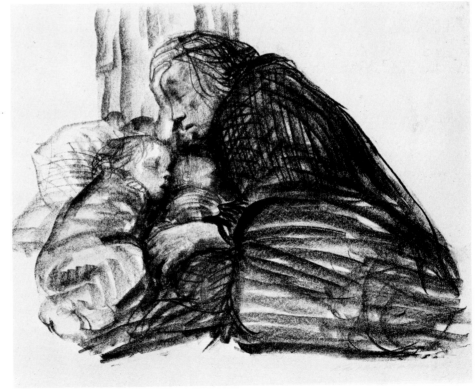

little, considering the standing she had. She was never greedy for money, but it worried her that her husband worked too hard, unable to let up because of the demands of his practice.

Her sixtieth birthday, in 1927, brought many honors. Numerous exhibits of her work were held, notably one sponsored by the Prussian Academy of Arts. Articles appeared evaluating her work and worth. Tributes poured in from far and near, and she received and read personally between 400 and 500 letters.

Romain Rolland, in France, called her work the greatest German poem of her period. "This woman of manly heart," he declared, "has looked on [the poor], has taken them into her motherly arms with a solemn and tender compassion. She is the voice for the silence of those who have been sacrificed."

A new analytic catalogue of her graphic prints was published, including the work she had done since the previous catalogue in 1913. Her drawings, too, were in the collections of the leading museums of Germany.

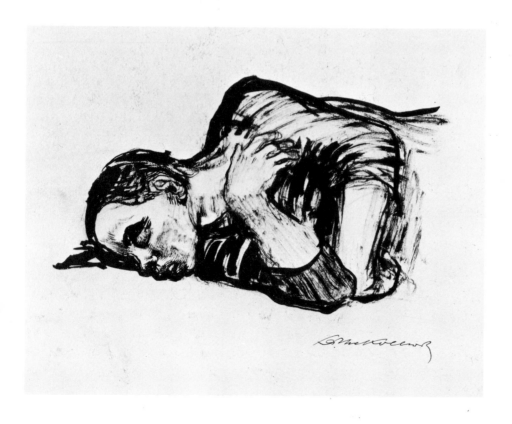

"Suicide" (*Selbstmord*) Drawing in India ink, of about 1926.

The artist contributed this drawing to a special issue of the periodical *Eulenspiegel* opposing the German government's decision to build a battleship.
Kunsthalle, Hamburg.

"The Agitator" (*Der Agitationsredner*) Lithograph, 1926.

This appeared as part of a picture series called *Types* (*Typen*) issued by the Germania Press of Leipzig, Germany. *Kunsthalle, Hamburg.*

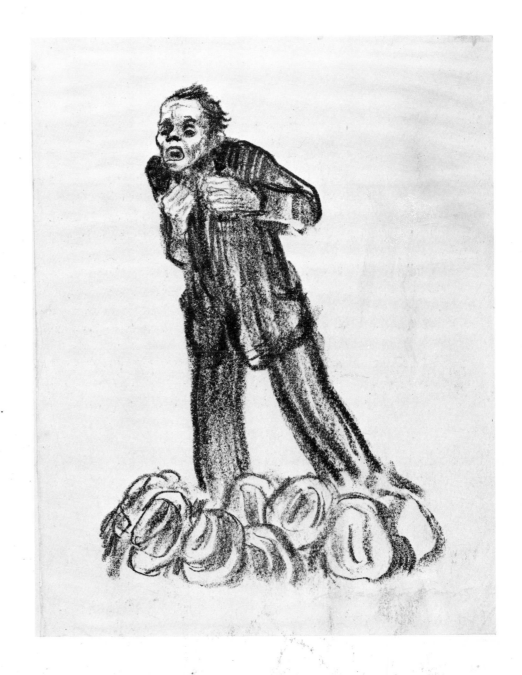

Perhaps the most impressive honor was an unofficial and even unintentional one. Since 1910 Ernst Barlach had lived and worked in the little town of Güstrow, Mecklenburg. In 1926 he sculpted the figure of a hovering angel for the cathedral there. That angel's face hauntingly suggests the face of Käthe Kollwitz. Barlach later told a friend that this face had come to him as he worked, without any deliberate decision on his part. "Had I planned it, it would never have come off."

93

From many sides messages, tributes, and appeals came to Käthe Kollwitz during these years in the Germany of the Weimar Republic. She received a constant stream of letters, most of them from strangers expressing approval, enthusiasm, even reverence for her work. Some asked her for advice to aid their careers. Should they go in for art? If so, what was the shortest, best route to follow? Others, often from would-be artists who assumed she must by now be wealthy from her own work, begged or even demanded money from her. There was even this kind of threat: "If I haven't received 300 marks from you by 2 P.M. next Friday, I'll commit suicide!"

A typewriter was now installed in the Kollwitz residence on Weissenburger Street. The artist hired a typist to come regularly and take dictation so that this unasked-for mail might be answered properly. Her old friend Jeep couldn't understand how Schmidt could bear to give so much of her precious time for these replies. Why not simply disregard most of them? Käthe Kollwitz, however, couldn't look the other way when human beings reached out to her, whether they came with praise for her art, in search of encouragement for their own, or to demand help, however unreasonably. She admitted, at the same time, that she felt somewhat like the child who wanted to go back into its mother's womb. "I'd like to be back again in the belly of being unknown, of living only for myself." She was far more acutely aware of the penalties than of the prestige and sparkle associated with fame.

Though she responded faithfully to her unmet art public, Käthe Kollwitz almost never frequented fashionable restaurants, coffeehouses, or night spots where prominent artists, writers, publishers, and other intellectuals of Berlin gathered to see and be seen. The best known of such spots was the Romanische Café, a coffeehouse in the Viennese style located in Berlin's fashionable West End. The Romanische, as the café was called for short, stood in the very shadow of the Kaiser Wilhelm Memorial Church, a pseudo-Romanesque landmark erected by Kaiser Wilhelm II to honor his predecessor and to indulge his own conviction that he had a rare talent for architecture. (A similar illusion was to be shared to an even greater extent by Adolf Hitler.)

At the Romanische, artists might meet dealers or even patrons, writers might find publishers, actors and playwrights might make contact with critics or producers, and one and all could hope to encounter some journalist who might get them favorable mention in the daily press or magazines. It was, in fact, a kind of unofficial career exchange. The steady patrons of the Romanische included a good many dilettantes and poseurs, but also some very solid and influential personalities. Often seen there, for example, were the painter Max Slevogt and the publisher Bruno Cassirer. (The great Paul Cassirer, mentioned earlier, died in 1926.) Even the eminent, urbane, and witty Max Liebermann (1847–1935), the dean of Germany's living painters, was sometimes to be found at the Romanische.

During all of some fourteen years of growing recognition and reputation in Weimar Germany (1919–1933), Käthe Kollwitz was seen at the Romanische not more than once or twice. A small but revealing report of one such visit tells how she and Dr. Karl Kollwitz, having traveled from their north Berlin residence more to see this place than to be seen there, sat quietly and unobtrusively at one of the small tables of the café. They were not awkward or timid, but obviously they were not at home amidst the glib, wisecracking, sophisticated regulars of the Romanische.

That kind of world was not for her, nor she for it. The sort of recognition it brought meant almost nothing to her. Her roots ran too deep to permit her to sway in the gusty breezes of fads or fashions. Stability, almost to the extent of stubbornness, had become her hallmark. Her important relationships in life were long-lasting: a lifelong marriage, an ever-growing closeness to her younger sister Lise, the enduring friendship with Jeep, her contacts with her surviving son Hans and his family, and even the half-century-long relationship with her housekeeper, Lina Mäkler, now known respectfully as "Fräulein Lina."

Coordinated with and crowning all these continuities and loyalties was her lifelong dedication to her art. Periods came when she forged ahead at an accelerated rate; at other times, things went slowly, seeming almost to halt; but it was never conceivable to her that she could live without her work—not as long as she remained able to hold a crayon or a pen and make it bring into being on paper what she saw with her extraordinary inner vision.

In 1927 Käthe Kollwitz and her husband received an invitation to visit the Soviet Union, then celebrating the tenth anniversary of the Russian Revolution. Several other German artists and writers were likewise to be guests.

On her arrival in Moscow Käthe Kollwitz proved as usual to be reserved and even shy in meeting with her Soviet hosts and colleagues. How-

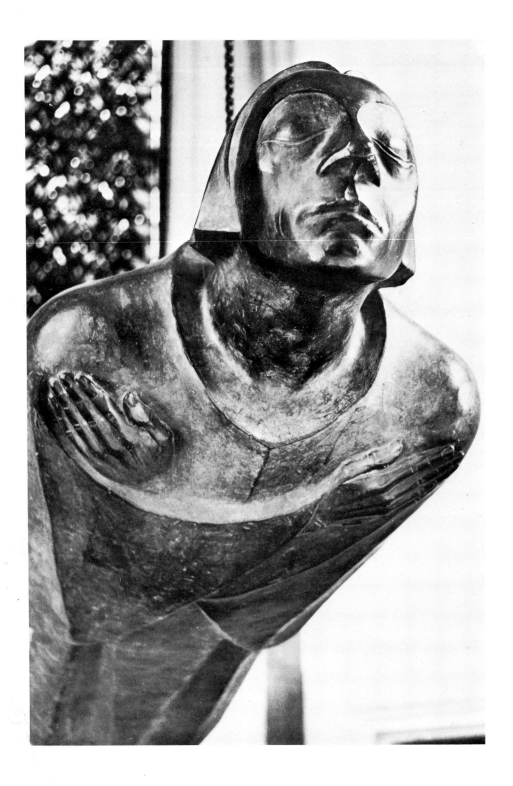

The bronze angel by Barlach, with a face like that of Käthe Kollwitz. This now hangs, suspended as if in mid-air, in the fourteenth-century Antoniter Church, in Cologne. This hovering angel has become well known in Germany. It is regarded as a symbol or personification of lamentation over the battlefields of the two world wars.
Tourist Bureau, City of Cologne.

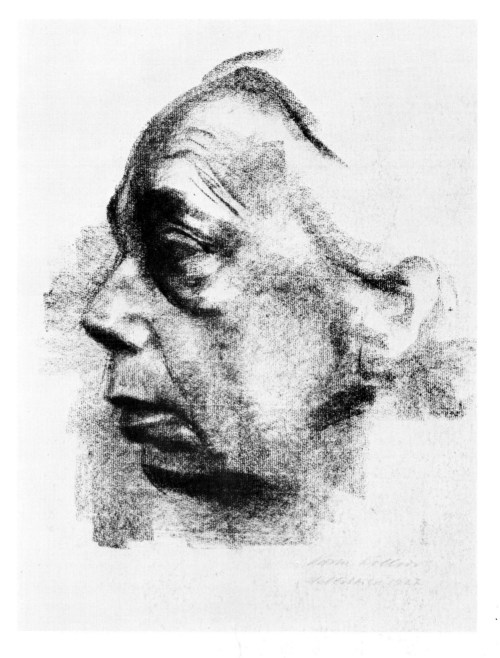

"Self-portrait" (*Selbstbildnis*)
Lithograph, 1927. The original
size was about 12½ × 11¼
inches.
*Fogg Art Museum, Harvard
University.*

ever she visited the tomb of Lenin, leader of the Revolution, who had died
only three years before. She stood gazing at Lenin's form for a quarter of
an hour as if engaged in a silent dialogue.

Confrontation with the mortal remains of significant people seemed to
fascinate her. She had viewed and drawn the body of the assassinated Karl
Liebknecht in 1919. Now in 1927 it was Lenin. And in dark days of the
1930s it was to be the body of an artist of especial importance to her, Ernst
Barlach.

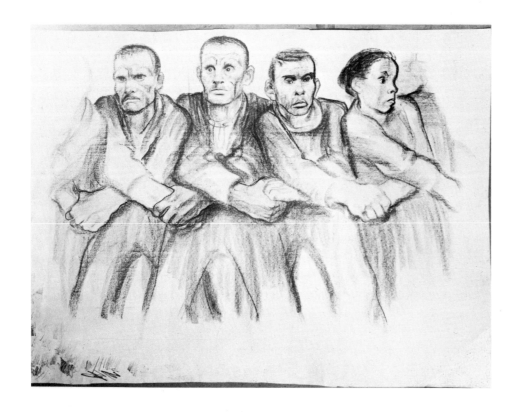

"Solidarity—The Propeller Song" (*Solidarität—Das Propellerlied*) Lithograph, 1931–1932.

The words of the popular "Propeller Song" included the line, "We protect the Soviet Union."

The original size was about 22 × 32¾ inches. The lithographic stone has been destroyed. Relatively few prints were made from it. *Deutsche Fotothek Dresden.*

In Russia she showed herself, typically, most moved by the plight of myriads of children whose lives had been uprooted during the Revolution. Whole villages had stood deserted while neglected, hungry children poured like swarms of locusts over the land, seeking refuge in the cities. By the time of the Kollwitz visit in 1927 many of these children had been placed in homes and were being trained for trades. The artist and her husband saw one of the carpentry workshops where such training went on. She noted also that one of these "wild children" had been adopted by Clara Zetkin, a German Communist leader and associate of Lenin. But the boy had escaped and gone back again to the road.

Years later, during the early period of Nazi rule in Germany, the artist recalled these Russian children in writing to a friend who had emigrated to Israel and was working with children there. Always she was moved most immediately by what concerned the welfare of children.

Her visit to the Soviet Union led to the creation of "The Listeners," a lithograph based on a sketch made during a celebration in Moscow. In the spring of 1932 appeared her poster sometimes called "Solidarity," sometimes "The Propeller Song," which was made in response to a request she had received from Russian artists. It bears the inscription "We Protect the Soviet Union." Not many years later, Russian soldiers and guerrillas were protecting their land against millions of Hitler's invading soldiers, including the grandson of this same artist.

Besides creating posters for causes near and dear to her, she was commissioned to illustrate books by the French authors Romain Rolland and Henri Barbusse (1873?–1935); the Germans Arno Holz (1863–1929) and Heinrich Mann (1871–1950), and the American Jack London (1876–1916). Such assignments, coming from the outside, seemed to stimulate her creativity.

The 1927–1928 period included her only work on a biblical subject— first a drawing, then a sequence of three woodcuts, all called "Mary and Elizabeth." They depict the meeting and mutual recognition of the two future mothers: Elizabeth, pregnant with John the Baptist, and Mary, pregnant with Jesus, as told in the Gospel of St. Luke 1:5–80.

This most maternal theme had come to Käthe Kollwitz first from an anonymous painting of the mid-fifteenth century that she had seen exhibited in Berlin during 1922. Otherwise her art, varied though it is, contains little of formal religion. A deeply moving sculpture of 1938 is called "Pietà," the traditional name for works showing Mary holding the dead body of her son, Jesus. But Kollwitz indicated by a specific comment that she had not here depicted Divine beings; rather this mother was a lonely old woman darkly brooding over mankind's rejection of her son. A 1923 drawing, "Death Bends over a Woman," seems to show a crown of thorns beside the figures. Other than these suggestions, any religious content in the work of Käthe Kollwitz is implied rather than stated directly.

In the spring of 1928 the artist became a civil servant of the state of Prussia, largest political unit in the Germany of the time. She was appointed during that April to supervise advanced students—also called master students —in graphics for the Prussian Academy of Arts, and in May she took the traditional oath of office. She had for some time been awaiting final word on this appointment. Her hope was that when she had a steady salary plus the studio provided by the Academy, her husband could give up his overly strenuous work for the health insurance fund. Her monthly net salary was modest enough—less than 880 marks, roughly $220 at the rates of exchange then prevailing.

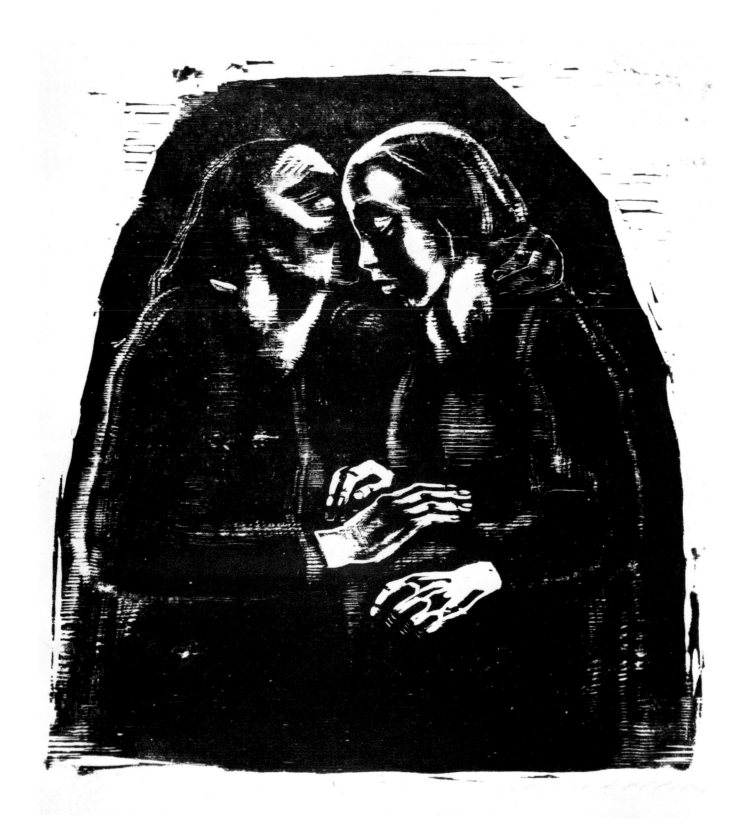

This small step toward security did not prevent her, in the autumn of 1928, from joining other progressive artists and intellectuals in signing a public protest against the German government's decision to build a battle cruiser —a step toward the old armaments race.

In the studio provided for her by the Academy, Professor Kollwitz continued her work on the figures of the mourning parents for the soldiers' memorial to which she had so long been dedicated.

May 1929 brought her a new public honor—the Prussian award entitled *Pour le Mérite,* which dated back to Frederick the Great. Originally a military award only, it was also given for outstanding merit in the arts and sciences after 1842.

That same month of May was marred by new bloodshed and bitterness as the Prussian police brutally crushed protest gatherings by radical workers in the streets of Berlin. It was a disturbing time for the Kollwitzes.

In 1930 the artist was not well. She limited her activities but gave her available energy to her art. Germany, too, was deeply ailing. The economic depression grew worse. Unemployment increased catastrophically. Hunger spread. Taxes were high. A coalition government had collapsed, and complex political deals and maneuvers went on behind the scenes.

In the elections of September 1930 the Nazis—Hitler's fascist National Socialist Party—showed alarming strength. It became second largest of the many parties in the national parliament, or Reichstag, where it was exceeded only by the Social Democratic Party with which the Kollwitz family was connected.

"Evil reaction is creeping into all areas," wrote the artist before the end of 1930. She mentioned the ban against the showing of the film *All Quiet on the Western Front,* made from the well-known antiwar novel by Erich Maria Remarque, a German novelist. "A bad time is coming, or is now here."

She noted, too, that unemployment was widespread not only in Germany but on all continents of the world.

A bad time indeed, but worse ones were ahead. As artist and concerned citizen Käthe Kollwitz saw the way things were moving. In the German state of Thuringia the Nazis had come to power and quickly acted to purge modern art works from the collection in Weimar, a city closely identified with the lives of Goethe and Schiller. In the trade school of Weimar a wall painting by a modern artist was ordered destroyed. Even earlier, the famous Bauhaus design school had been forced out of Weimar by reactionary and

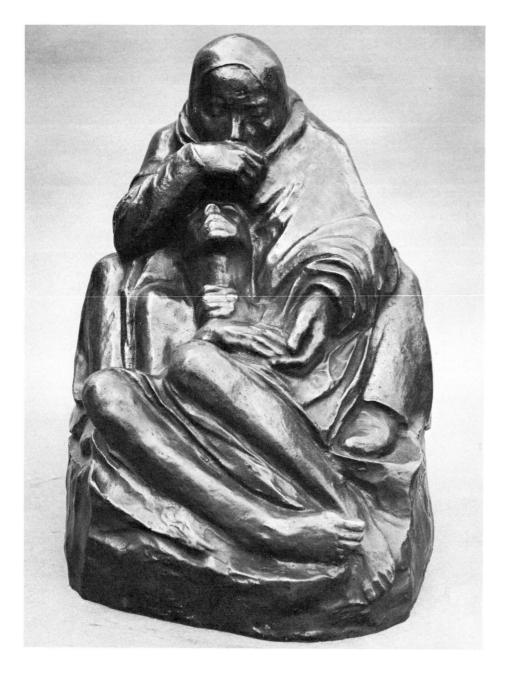

"Pietà" Bronze statue, 1937–1938. Dimensions are about 14⅞ × 11¼ × 15¼ inches. *Photograph by courtesy of Marlborough Fine Art (London)Ltd.*

nationalist pressures. It moved to Dessau only to be expelled from there also in 1932 when the Nazis came to power in the state of Anhalt-Dessau.

As more and more millions became jobless, hungry, and desperate, appeals plastered on billboards repeatedly showed the powerful Kollwitz poster of 1924, "Germany's Children Are Hungry." Yet the reactionary far right, financed by some of the wealthiest industrialists and bankers, mounted increasing attacks not only on modern art and literature in general, but even

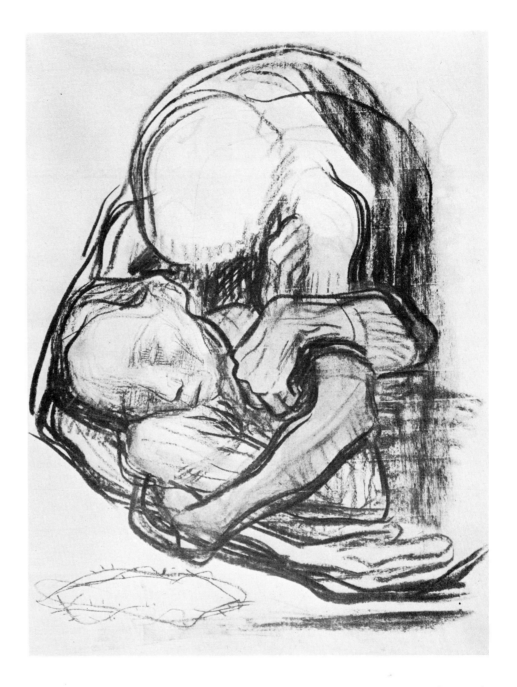

"Death Bends over a Woman"
(*Der Tod beugt sich zu einer
Frau*) Charcoal drawing, 1923.
One of the series known as
Parting and Death (*Abschied
und Tod*).
Deutsche Fotothek Dresden.

on the humanitarianism that Käthe Kollwitz represented. One such attack declared, "We see Cultural Bolshevism in the sub-humanities of Kollwitz . . . [and] Barlach. . . ."

In her art she responded to the new problems and conflicts of the time. One of her two lithographs called "Demonstration" appeared in May 1931 in the *AIZ* (Workers' Illustrated Newspaper), a lively periodical of the left. Such demonstrations were on the increase. Those called by the Communists

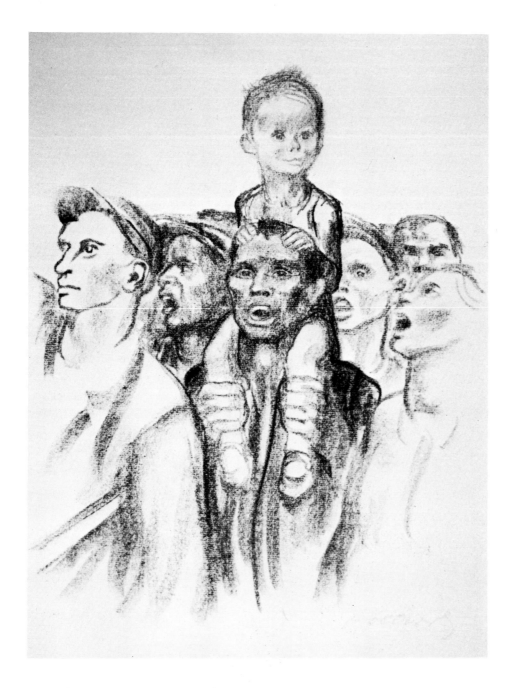

seemed to be broken up more swiftly and savagely by the police than those of the Nazis and ultranationalists. The courts commonly acted with similar bias.

Meanwhile, as if to remind herself of the warmth of human relationships amidst all the distress and rising horror, Käthe Kollwitz drew some of her tenderest, most appealing pictures of mothers and children.

Again and again her name appeared with names of other artists and

104

writers—warning, protesting, and appealing for resistance to the mounting trend toward fascism. In October 1931 she was listed among sponsors of a series of exhibitions called Artists in the Class Struggle, arranged by the Society of Revolutionary Artists in Germany. She loaned both her presence and her name when she thought they might help to stem the dark tides she saw sweeping in.

During 1931 a courageous antimilitarist journalist and editor, Carl von Ossietski, was sentenced to a year and a half in prison for writing an allegedly treasonable article in the weekly *Weltbühne*. At that time he said—and this was more than a year before Hitler was named chancellor—"It is not so bad, because there's really not much freedom in Germany. Gradually the differences between those who are imprisoned and those who aren't are fading out." (After the Nazis came to power, Ossietski, still imprisoned, was awarded the Nobel Peace Prize, and not many years later was brutally murdered while still incarcerated in a Nazi concentration camp.)

In the midst of these darkening days Käthe Kollwitz managed somehow

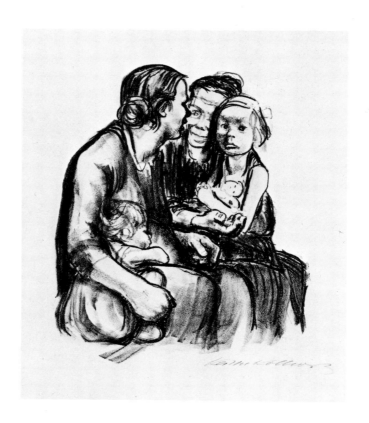

"Two Gossiping Women with Two Children" (*Zwei schwatzende Frauen mit zwei Kindern*) Lithograph, 1930. *Kunsthalle, Hamburg.*

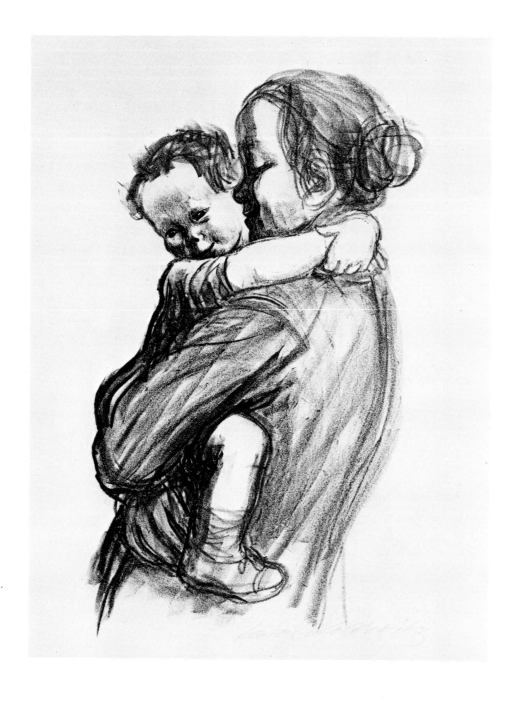

"Mother with Boy" (*Mutter mit Jungen*) Lithograph, 1931. Also known as "The Happy Mother." The size of the original is about 14 × 8½ inches. *Fogg Art Museum, Harvard University.*

to make progress on the most demanding and prolonged of her many self-imposed tasks. By the spring of 1931 she finished the two plaster figures for the memorial to her son Peter and the other dead soldiers. No one, not even her husband or her son Hans, had been allowed to see them while she worked. Finally, beginning April 22, 1931, they were placed on view at the Prussian Academy of Arts—a monumental, somber, heartbroken, and heart-

"Maternal Happiness" (*Mutterglück*) Lithograph, 1931.

The size of the picture on the lithographic stone, now destroyed, was about 9 × 12½ inches. The first edition of prints was made for a nonprofit association in Leipzig, The Aid for German Pictorial Art (*Deutsche Bildkunst-Hilfe*). *Staatliche Museen zu Berlin.*

breaking pair; the "Mourning Parents" could be recognized as Käthe and Karl Kollwitz themselves.

The visiting public and the art critics were enthusiastic. Otto Nagel, one of her friends among the revolutionary artists in Berlin, wrote, "They were the art sensation of the day. Never have I seen Käthe Kollwitz so excited." There was reason enough for her excitement. The two figures represented more than fifteen years of intense work. She herself called them a large section of her life and a most meaningful part of it. Some comments compared her with Constantin Meunier, the graphic artist she herself much admired, who had also turned successfully to sculpture late in life.

The plaster figures had still to be converted to stone before they could be placed outdoors in the soldiers' cemetery. The artist herself worked closely

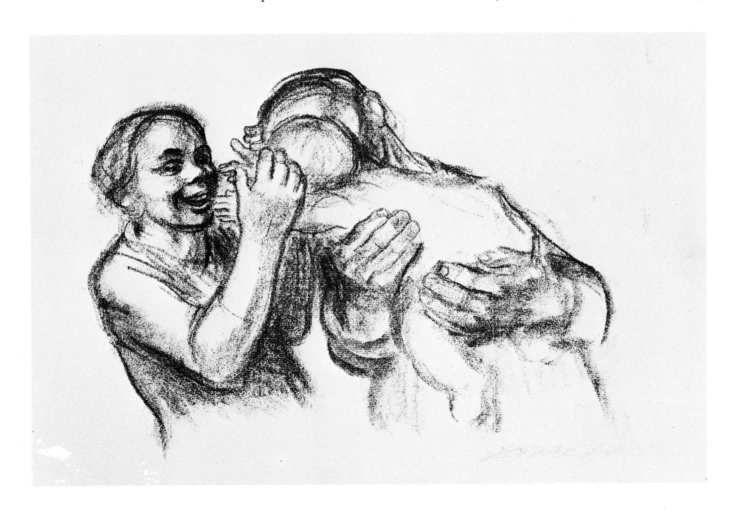

with two stone sculptors: Diederichs for the mourning mother figure, Rades for the father. Within a year, two figures of larger-than-life size had been completed in Belgian granite. It was not a true granite, but nevertheless a beautiful, blue-gray stone, less hard to work with and very durable, as the artist herself noted. She was deeply concerned that the figures should endure.

Financial as well as technical problems had to be met. Only 5,000 marks were given to support the project by the governments of the state of Prussia and the German Republic together. The cost of the stone and the fees of the two masons came to at least 6,000 marks, and then there were inevitable additional expenses for preparing the foundations at the site and for moving the stone figures to them.

The Kollwitzes were even prepared to dig into their own savings just so that ". . . they [the figures] will be there." There was reason behind this sense of urgency. The threat of total fascism in Germany was constantly increasing. "Let us hope that the Third Reich does not explode around us in the meantime. I am just as happy that the figures are made of granite," wrote Käthe Kollwitz, aware that Nazi hoodlums might seek to deface or shatter works of art that expressed antiwar sentiments.

Finally she secured some welcome concessions. The administration of the soldiers' cemetery in Belgium would provide the foundations and bases. In addition the usual Belgian tolls and transport charges would be waived.

Before they finally left Berlin the new stone figures were shown to the public in the entrance hall of the National Gallery. As their plaster originals had done, they won praise from critics writing for the leading newspapers and journals. But from one sector there came only a silence, which, the artist wrote in her diary on June 1, 1932, ". . . sickens or irritates me." The influential and important Communist papers had made no mention of the showing. She noted that she had heard of only one exception—a small comment in the central Communist paper, *Rote Fahne*, to the effect that ". . . one misses the antiwar gesture . . ." in the memorial figures. To her diary she entrusted her only protest: ". . . that is . . . downright stupid." But the comment also seemed to her to be damaging, for ". . . the broad masses of the working class are not coming . . . ," and she wanted their attendance above all. She wished that her friend Otto Nagel were in Berlin because he would not have tolerated this treatment.

Nagel, however, was then in the Soviet Union, holding showings of more than 140 important Kollwitz pictures. They attracted admiration and praise there—first in Moscow, then in Leningrad. Käthe Kollwitz wrote to

Nagel from Berlin telling of her partial disappointment, but giving news also of the general success. The two-week exhibition at the National Gallery had to be extended a week to accommodate the crowds.

At long last the figures were placed in the Roggevelde cemetery during July 1932. Käthe and Karl Kollwitz were present, and they went then from the stone figures to the grave of their son Peter. "Everything," she wrote, "was alive and felt to the utmost."

Then she stood again before her stone figure of the mother. "I . . . looked at her, my own face, and wept and stroked her cheeks. Karl stood close behind me. I had not known it. I heard him whispering, 'Yes, yes.' How close we were then!"

Completion of the memorial to the war dead proved like the lifting of a great weight from the artist's spirits. Her old friend Jeep, seeing her shortly after the figures were finished, found her surprisingly changed, seemingly younger and fresher. Her self-imposed task, or penance, had been fulfilled.

Yet only a short time before she had been depressed and ill. Her doctor son, Hans, had even recommended a psychotherapist, a woman who visited Käthe and suggested that she begin a course of treatment. The artist was doubtful that such treatment could dispel her depression but was asked to think it over. Her work seems to have been the only therapy that followed.

Shortly after her return from Belgium to Berlin she received a letter congratulating her on her sixty-fifth birthday. It came from a prisoner serving time for resisting military service. She wrote him a warm, friendly reply. In it she told sadly of the soldiers' cemeteries in Belgium with their endless rows of crosses marking the graves of the dead from many countries. But near the old battlefields of 1914–1918 she had seen a tower whose four sides carried the pledge

NEVER AGAIN WAR!

in four languages: German, Flemish, French, and English.

"You bolster this creed by going to prison," she wrote. "I greet you joyfully for what you have done."

The rules of the state of Prussia called for civil servants to retire when they passed the age of sixty-five. But the artist had prepared for this. With the help of friends, including the great old painter Max Liebermann, now honorary president of the Prussian Academy of Arts, she succeeded in securing a special reappointment under a contract. There were delays, but by mid-

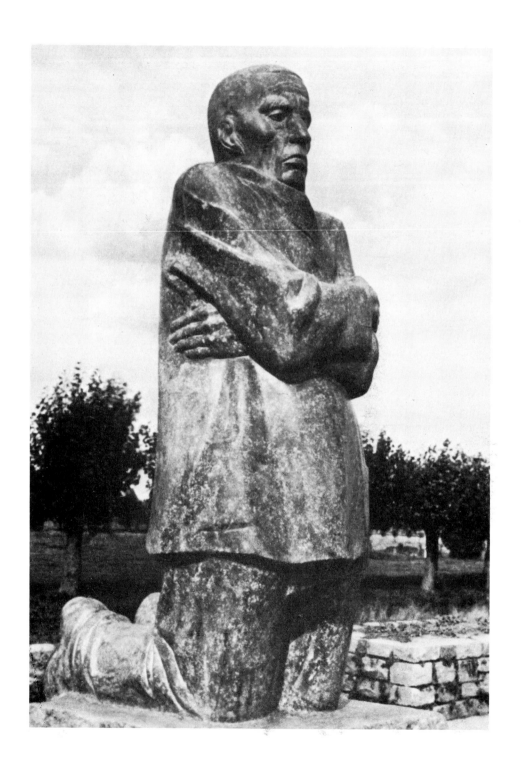

"The Mourning Father" converted to stone, standing at the soldiers' cemetery near Roggevelde, Belgium. Its height, from the base to the top of the head, is about 59½ inches. *Deutsche Fotothek Dresden.*

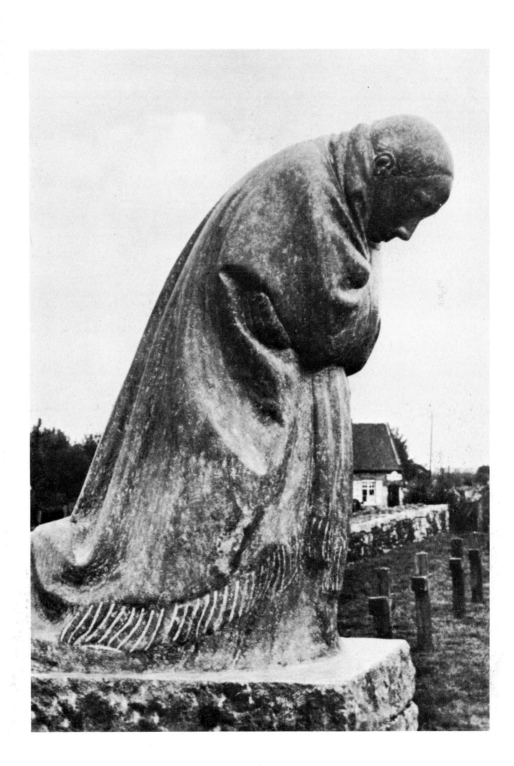

"The Mourning Mother" in stone, standing at the soldiers' cemetery near Roggevelde, Belgium. The features here are obviously and explicitly based on those of the artist herself. The height of the figure, from the base to the top of the head is about 48 inches. *Deutsche Fotothek Dresden.*

August 1932 it was arranged, albeit with a reduction in her small salary.

Only gifted and accomplished people were accepted as the artist's master pupils at the Prussian Academy. A teacher of her standing was expected to work with no more than two such master students at a time. However, the surviving Academy records indicate that at least five students—three women and two men—worked thus under Professor Kollwitz.

One of these, Elizabeth Voigt, born in 1898, studied for a relatively long time with the artist, who supplied a handwritten certificate of accomplishments when her pupil graduated from the Art Academy (*Kunsthochschule*) of Berlin in autumn 1935. By that time the Nazis had ousted Käthe Kollwitz as teacher and as member of the Prussian Academy of Arts, but she testified nevertheless that Fräulein Voigt had solid achievements in graphics, especially in woodcutting.

One of Elizabeth Voigt's cherished keepsakes was an autographed photo showing her teacher at work on a small statue. The indications are that this picture was taken in 1934 or 1935. With Fräulein Voigt and her other students Käthe Kollwitz maintained close and helpful relations, not only when they were officially listed as her pupils, but also afterward—even when, as in some cases, they were obliged to emigrate after the Nazi takeover in Germany.

During 1932 that country continued on its downward course. Chancellors followed, one after another—Heinrich Brüning, Franz von Papen, Kurt von Schleicher—and leaders of the older right-wing parties sought to build bulwarks against breakdown, first without, then finally with, Adolf Hitler's "help." His fierce and demagogic attacks on the Weimar Republic, the Versailles Treaty, the Communists, the Socialists, and the Jews attracted to his Nazi party the confused, the disgruntled, the desperate, and the alienated of whom there were many in Germany.

As the President, ex-General Paul von Hindenburg, declined into senility, his intimates and advisers urged him to support dictatorial reaction and, finally, fascism. Easter 1932 was, as the artist noted in her diary, not a time of hope but of ". . . misery! The dark misery into which the people are sinking. The loathsome political incitements!"

Prior to the Reichstag elections of July 31, 1932, she and her husband gave their names to an appeal urging supporters of both the Socialist and the Communist parties to join forces, work together, and outvote the Nazis. The

"Self-portrait in Bronze" (*Selbstbildnis, Bronze*) Sculpture, 1926–1936. Its actual size is about 9 inches from side to side, and 14½ inches from top to bottom.
Photograph by courtesy of Dr. Hans Kollwitz and Marlborough Fine Art (London) Ltd.

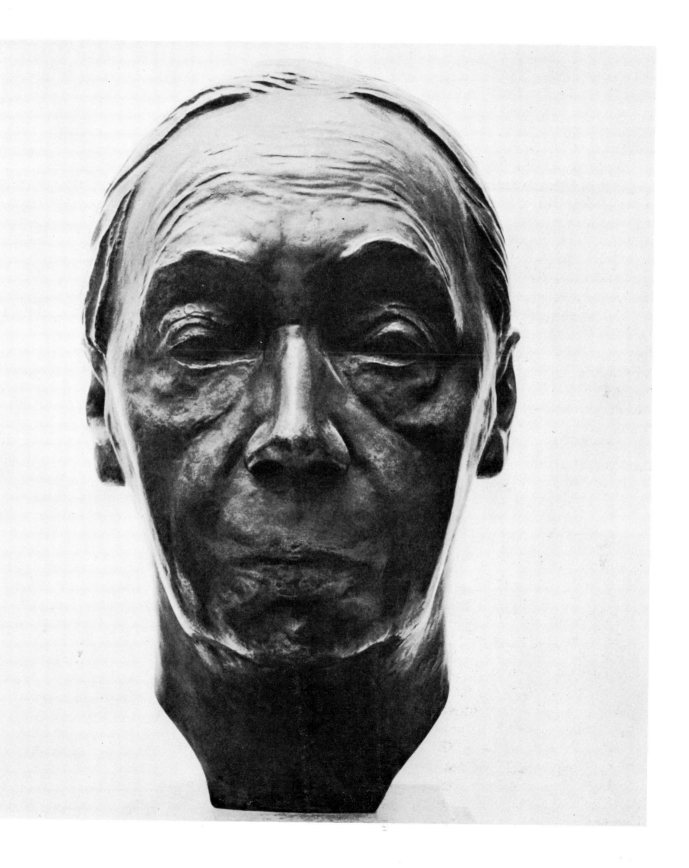

thirty-five signers of this appeal included also Heinrich Mann and Albert Einstein.

Around this sad time death again visited the Kollwitz family circle. Käthe's brother, Konrad Schmidt, had worked for years as a journalist for the Socialist Party's daily, the *Vorwärts*, and then had been given a position as a university teacher. In 1925 he was widowed by the sudden death of his wife, Anna. Bereft and bewildered he had been taken into the Kollwitz household. "He is very helpless and alone," Käthe wrote. Konrad's physical and psychological decline went far. Finally the once brilliant young socialist intellectual and writer had become a senile, pitiable remnant. Clearly the only release for him lay in death. It came to him at last in that autumn of 1932.

As always Käthe found through her art effective outlet for the deeply moving events or insights of her life. In haunting drawings and lithographs she reflected her brother's last days. One of these, entitled "Konrad Calls to Death," shows the old man half rising from his chair as he seeks to catch at a passing cloak—clearly part of the garments of Death personified. A few strokes only—a foot and some draperies—are drawn to suggest Death, but those few suffice.

Käthe Kollwitz brooded repeatedly on the handicaps that often come with old age. Inwardly she rebelled against them. She wanted always to remain well and alert enough to keep on working.

chapter 8
1933-1938

Hitler's Third Reich Arrives with Complete Dictatorship

"The Third Reich has broken out," Käthe Kollwitz recorded ominously in her diary.

On January 30, 1933, Adolf Hitler was appointed Chancellor of Germany by President von Hindenburg, and the debacle began. Gradually at first, then with ever-quickening and sickening speed, Hitler and his cohorts seized control of every facet of German life and expression. Repression and terror soon became the order of the day and of the night. "Arrests and house searches," the artist noted, "complete dictatorship."

Beginning in February large numbers of prominent radical artists, writers, and antiwar leaders had to flee Germany. The anti-Nazi artists who remained were ousted from positions they held and denied the right to show or sell their works. Jewish artists, including some leading figures in the art world, were most bitterly persecuted, even being ordered to stop painting and drawing.

A week before Hitler was named Chancellor, Ernst Barlach had talked on the radio, indignantly asserting the independence of artists against the growing Nazi threat. And shortly after Hitler became Chancellor, Käthe Kollwitz and the venerable Max Liebermann were among those who voted to award Barlach the Prussian order *Pour le Mérite*.

Still more courageous—or rash—she and her husband joined Heinrich Mann and other prominent personalities in another appeal to all workers, Socialist or Communist, for electoral unity against the Nazis and reactionaries. New Reichstag elections had been set for March 5.

For three days their appeal was publicly displayed. It urged united action in order that "... inertia and cowardice should not allow Germany to sink into barbarism!" Then came the sensational fire in the Reichstag building, the unleashing of open Nazi terror, and the scrapping of almost all remaining civil rights. The appeal for united action against German fascism had been in vain.

The new Nazi Minister for Education, who held power over all forms of artistic expression in Prussia, was a psychotic ex-schoolteacher, Dr. Bernhard Rust. Through him came the threat that the Prussian Academy of Arts would be closed unless Käthe Kollwitz and Heinrich Mann, the novelist, were removed from its roster of members. They were forced to resign.

The purging of Käthe Kollwitz from the Academy was like a knell sounding the death of the fine-arts policies of the Weimar Republic, which Hitler was now swiftly strangling. Despite its manifold shortcomings and inadequacies, Weimar Germany had at least provided freedom for artists in many areas: drama, music, pictorial arts. In his excellent *Germany—A Modern History* (1961), Marshall M. Dill wrote that the "... unique contribution of Weimar Germany to painting was the school of expressionism, much of which ... involved piercing social criticism of bourgeois society." He added, "Perhaps the work that will endure longest is the extraordinarily compassionate drawing of Käthe Kollwitz whose delineation of the poor and downtrodden in their misery is unique."

Late in February 1933, the artist wrote a friend that she was so gripped by the unheard of political events that she could not work, though she went daily to her studio. She feared that extremely difficult and bloody times were ahead. "No," she wrote, "they are already here ... each day brings more evil. Everything else seems insignificant."

Although she had lost her Academy membership and teaching position, her salary and the use of her Academy studio were allowed to continue until October. She told her old friend Jeep that she was overjoyed by this, for in that studio stood her large clay sculpture group "Protecting Mother," and she had nowhere else to take it if she were evicted.

For the time being, despite the ban on her teaching, she continued to help her master students, and the Secretary of the Academy looked the other way. She tried, at intervals, to adjust inwardly to the upheavals. "The wave carried me up," she is said to have remarked, "now it carries me down again."

In mid-March she and her husband on advice of friends went to the spa of Marienbad, Czechoslovakia, ostensibly for a two-week vacation. People

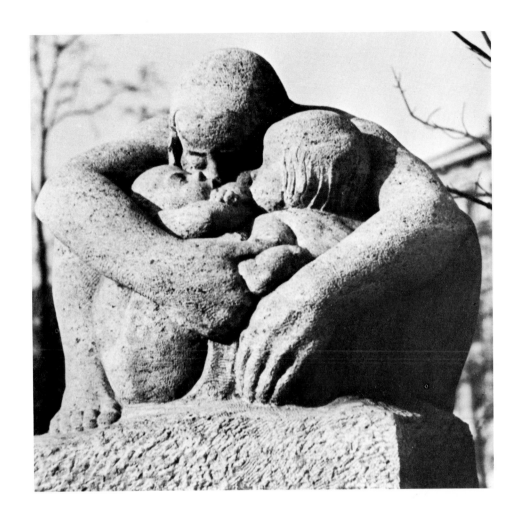

"Protecting Mother" or "Mother Group" (*Muttergruppe*) Sculpture in limestone. As shown here, it had been placed on a base in the Berlin park now called Kollwitz Platz. Approximate height of the sculpture is 30 inches. *Deutsche Fotothek Dresden.*

were then allowed by law to take only a few German marks out of the country. Karl Kollwitz took more—but only some fifty marks. His lifelong honesty stood him in bad stead at this time. Yet even if they had been bolder or more rash, the Kollwitzes were not inwardly ready to attempt flight to another country. Their son, their grandchildren, their friends, their work, their roots—all remained in Germany.

From Marienbad, the artist wrote Jeep that it seemed everyone was now withdrawing, hiding like a snail deep in his own shell. She and Karl intended to return soon to Berlin. But this time she was not happy at the prospect. The new stifling atmosphere in Germany was impossible to escape; one awoke in it, one went to sleep in it. She was worried, too, for her son. "Perhaps they will bother [Hans] . . . ." The letter was signed with wry humor, "Your subdued snails, Käthe and Karl."

In a letter to a young friend about six weeks after their return to Berlin, she wrote of the impossibility of real rest in Germany. But still she wanted ". . . to work as much as I can and as well as I can."

Meanwhile, in rapid succession, the Nazi leaders launched boycotts of Jewish merchants, seized and crushed Germany's great trade union organizations, burned books by writers of whom they disapproved, and then wiped out every political party but their own. By mid-1933 Hitler's organization and the German state were one. Germany's Weimar Constitution was a shattered relic. Pacifism, liberalism, democracy were hunted down. Within about three years the Nazi dictatorship also made complete its control over art and artists in Germany.

In May 1933 Max Liebermann was forced to resign his honorary presidency of the Academy of Arts. In his behalf as well as that of Käthe Kollwitz, Ernst Barlach wrote to the Academy's president, composer Max von Schillings. Such protests were in vain. Barlach himself soon became the victim of the full blacklist treatment. Otto Nagel, who knew the Kollwitzes well, said that Käthe was more stricken by what was done to Barlach than by her own difficulties.

Many Germans who had been especially active against the Nazis fled, if they could, into other lands. Paris became one important center of anti-Nazi refugees. By mid-1933 presses there were pouring out copies of *The Brown Book*, an exposé of events in the Hitler Reich. It had been quickly prepared by refugee writers under the leadership of Willi Münzenberg, who had been until a few months earlier the most dynamic force in the Communist press of Germany.

"The senseless Nazi work of destruction proceeds in all areas of fine arts," this book declared. It warned that the Nazi line would make inevitable the exile of Käthe Kollwitz, the inspired artist of the world of workers.

Käthe was not personally banished but the time came all too soon when her works were banished from public view. Even that was never done by official announcement; after all, she was widely known and beloved. It was accomplished surreptitiously but efficiently.

During those nightmare months of May and June 1933 the artist revealed her clear view of the realities and also a considerable fortitude. Without her knowledge or wish, Jeep's husband, Arthur Bonus, had sent a futile letter to the notorious Hermann Goering, one of Hitler's specialists in violence, now top man in the state of Prussia. The letter urged that Frau Kollwitz be reinstated in the Academy of Arts. With it, to bolster this petition, went a copy of an article that Bonus had written for a religious publication stressing how dear she was to the hearts of masses of German workers. Goering made no response to this plea.

Preliminary proofs of that article reached Kollwitz. She begged at once that it not be published. In a revealing letter, she gave her reasons to Jeep. If, as the article said, countless workers now held her dear, they would assuredly cease to do so if she were to be honorably recognized by the Nazi regime. She would not herself crawl to get into the good graces of the new dictators, or—if she could prevent it—let others do so for her. "I want to, I must, stand by those who have been persecuted." Economic hardship, she knew, obviously must result from such a stand. But she would not be alone in suffering such disadvantages. Thousands were undergoing the same fate, and she had no right to lament her own share of it.

She continued with practical details. "I'll not [be able] to keep the studio in any case. After all, I'm a year past the age limit. Indeed, I regard the whole procedure against me as logical."

Beyond doubt if Käthe Kollwitz had kowtowed to the top Nazi leaders and completely altered her work to fit their wants and their propaganda they would have been more than willing to claim her as one of their true, great German artists. She could have bought her career and her position, as tens and hundreds of thousands of Germans did in those days, by selling out her convictions. This Käthe Kollwitz would not do. Indeed, she *could* not do it.

Even though some of her sculptures had been on public display in state galleries during the past months, she was not deceived. She knew this did not mean the new regime was relenting or softening toward her. The recent exhibitions of her work had been due solely to the presence of individual museum heads who respected her art and who had not yet been fired. New museum heads were being appointed, and new rules drafted. When these changes were completed, then ". . . we shall see whether I shall still exist."

She did continue for a time to exist in the shape of some of her sculptures that remained on view in a well-known museum on Unter den Linden, called the "Crown Prince Palace."

Kollwitz sculptures could still be seen there until the Nazi regime was more than three and a half years old and the foreign visitors to the Olympic Games of 1936 had left Berlin. Then, by order of Rust, the Crown Prince Palace museum was shut down. Soon afterward, early in 1937, Hitler and other leading Nazis got around to a complete crackdown on "degenerate art" all over Germany.

In a diary entry of October 1933 Käthe Kollwitz noted cryptically that "Gerhart Hauptmann says: Yes—and Kerr calls him a traitor." Reading between the lines, one can reconstruct what was implied here. Hauptmann, author of *The Weavers* and many other plays of social content, was the only German writer of note who capitulated to the Hitler regime and served it as effective window dressing. Alfred Kerr had been an influential drama critic and essayist in pre-Hitler Germany. His comment that Hauptmann was a traitor could hardly have been written or spoken openly in Germany after about March 1933. Käthe Kollwitz must in some way have learned— through channels or word of mouth—what Kerr had said about the dramatist she had admired.

Along with other doctors who had belonged to the Social Democratic Physicians Society, Dr. Karl Kollwitz was deprived of his health insurance practice during 1933. Nevertheless in this period he treated private patients in a small room he had arranged in the family apartment. After many months of gloom and uncertainty he and some other doctors were reinstated in November and, during good behavior, allowed to serve their regular patients again.

The Kollwitzes' son, Hans, also a doctor, was notified of his reinstatement as well. Nevertheless, the very evening of the day he learned this, September eighteenth, his home in Lichtenrade was searched by Nazis. They confiscated much of his mother's art as well as books of hers which had been taken there for greater safety. These seizures may well have been the purpose of the raid.

The Kollwitz family's troubles were complicated further because Karl had developed a serious eye ailment. He was operated on for cataracts, but the results were unsatisfactory. Nevertheless he insisted on continuing to visit his sick patients, climbing dark stairways by day or night. For a while he was assisted by a young doctor, and Hans often came to help out in the evenings.

The atmosphere in Germany at this time was one of suspicion, spying, denunciation, and terror. Käthe Kollwitz avoided unnecessary risks. If she wanted to talk with some freedom to a visitor in her home, she would pull out the telephone plug and block the opening with a wad of cotton to thwart any listening device. She was one of the many who knew that the dreaded Gestapo—secret state police—installed devices in telephones to pick up conversations even when the receiver was not off the hook.

When Fräulein Lina, her housekeeper of thirty years, entered the room the artist would often switch suddenly to another topic of conversation. She had no reason to distrust Lina, but one could never be careful enough in this stifling atmosphere of the Hitler Reich.

In November 1933 she visited the grave of her brother Konrad. "I laid down red carnations," she noted in her diary, "for him and for his dead Social Democracy." Both now seemed not only dead but distant.

In spite of much mental turmoil she tried to continue with her "Protecting Mother," a large maternal figure fiercely clutching two children to her body. Unable to complete it by the time the Academy studio had to be vacated, the artist sought and got permission to remain three months longer.

When she did move out of the studio there was no room at home for her art work and materials. But by October 1934 she had rented a place in a studio building on Kloster Street, near Berlin's well-known old Alexanderplatz. She was one of some forty artists in the building, many of whom were sympathetic to her. Working there on her sculpture now gratified and soothed her.

During the interim period when she had been unable to work on it, in the summer of 1934, she had gone back to graphics in her home and begun *Death*, her last great series of lithographs. More than seven years before that time she had noted in her diary, "I must make prints that deal with Death. Must, must, must!" That theme, she declared, was inexhaustible.

The year 1934 brought the death of Georg Stern, husband of her favorite sister, Lise. In view of the conditions prevailing in Germany, it was a great comfort for her sister that Käthe Kollwitz herself spoke at the commemorative services for Georg Stern. Her dignity and eloquence at that time made a deep impression on all her family and especially on her nieces. This was but one of a number of times the artist participated in memorial services during the Hitler period.

It was not easy to work. She was growing older, became tired more easily, needed ever longer periods of rest. Yet her imagination and inner drive had not dwindled. "One can live without work," she told Jeep, "but then life lacks strength and savor."

Her eight *Death* lithographs are strong and gripping. They contemplate the coming of death with fear or fascination but without flinching. Especially shattering is "Death Reaches into a Group of Children." It seems

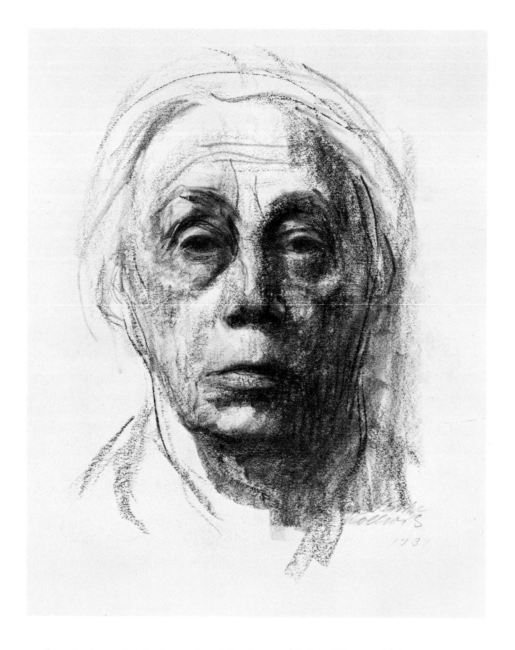

"Self-portrait" (*Selbstbildnis*) Charcoal and crayon drawing, 1934.

A magnificent study, made at the time the artist was preparing for one of her best-known lithographic self-portraits. *Los Angeles County Museum of Art, Los Angeles County Funds.*

to foreshadow death from the skies by aerial bombing, which was soon to overtake hundreds of thousands in Spain, in Poland, in the Netherlands, Britain, Russia, Germany, Japan, and elsewhere.

In the uncertain, confused November of 1934 she was invited to show her work at the Academy, the same from which she had been forced to resign. Always eager to see her art on exhibit, she accepted, and entered five of the lithographs from the *Death* cycle and one full-faced, haunting self-portrait, revealing what time and the times had done to her.

At this point an Academy of Arts official told her in confidence that

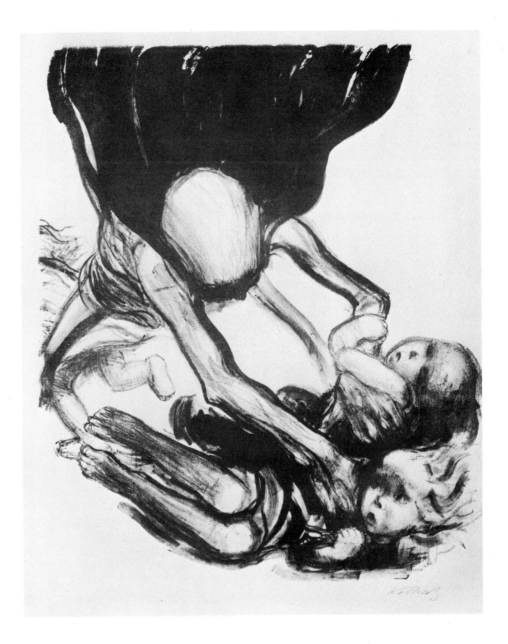

"Death Reaches into a Group of Children" (*Tod greift in Kinderschar*) Lithograph, 1934. This was the third print in the eight-print lithographic series called *Death* (*Tod*), all completed in the period 1934–1935.
*Kupferstichkabinett, Dresden.
Photograph taken by
Deutsche Fotothek Dresden.*

some supporters were maneuvering to have her readmitted to that institution. But she recorded in her diary a thought that became ever clearer to her: If readmission *should* be offered, "I must decline."

She was troubled as she prepared to exhibit her work under the Nazi regime. Even that, she felt, amounted to a kind of support. Also it smacked of disloyalty to good friends and colleagues who were now suffering ostracism, exile, and worse.

Outstanding among these because of his distinguished past was the painter—now ex-painter—Max Liebermann, accomplished, witty, politically

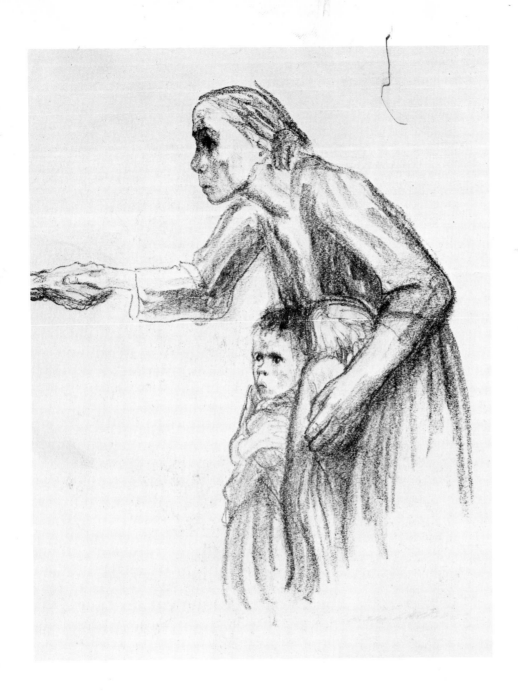

"Woman Entrusts Herself to Death" (*Frau vertraut sich dem Tode an*, sometimes also known as *Frau reicht dem Tod die Hand*) Lithograph, 1934. This was the first of the eight prints in the *Death* series. *Deutsche Fotothek Dresden.*

conservative—but a Jew. A fine artist, he had been a cofounder of the Berlin Secession, the active and able president of the Prussian Academy of Arts from 1920 to 1932, and its honorary president until the Hitler take-over. Now he and his wife were shunned by all but a few of those who before 1933 had sought their company and influence. A born Berliner, noted for his humor, Liebermann looked past his heavy curtains into the street where brown-clad Nazi storm troopers marched, and made a comment

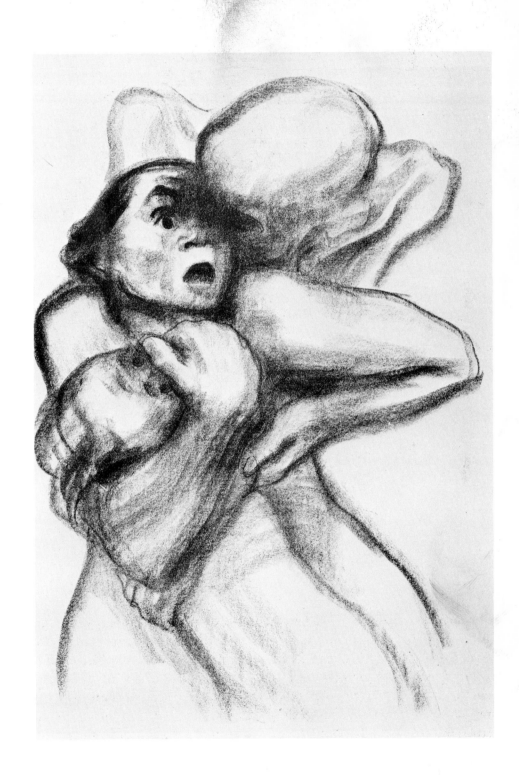

"Death Seizes a Woman" (*Tod
packt eine Frau*) Lithograph,
1934. This is the fourth print
in the *Death* series.
*Fogg Art Museum, Harvard
University.*

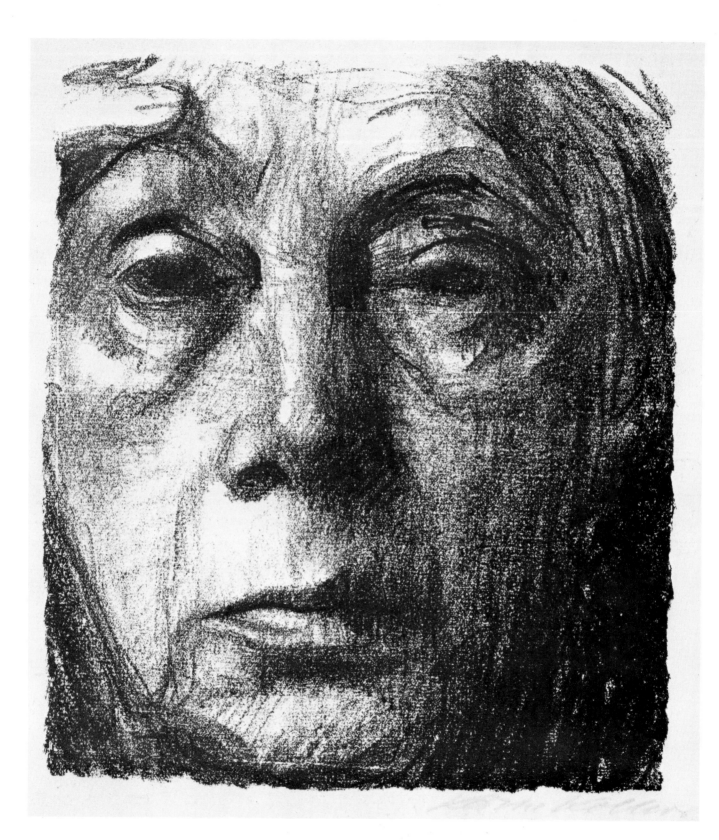

that was later repeated in endless whispered reports. "I can't eat as much as I'd like to vomit!"

Käthe Kollwitz confided to her diary that she wanted to call on Liebermann and ask him whether it was true that he had been ordered officially to cease all artistic activity, and whether the same order had gone also to Eugene Spiro, another eminent artist, for eighteen years head of the Berlin Secession group. The rumor was true in both these cases as well as others.

Finally she did call on the Liebermanns. But by that time it was too late for explanations or discussions. She found the old painter sick and swiftly declining, broken by persecution and isolation. Early in February 1935 he died at the age of eighty-eight.

Käthe Kollwitz paid a condolence call at the Liebermann residence, where she looked at the wasted body of her old friend and sponsor. She was one of only two non-Jews who attended the memorial service held for him by the Jewish Committee of Berlin. When his body was buried in the Jewish cemetery, she was one of four non-Jews from the art world who stood beside the grave. The other three who thus honored Liebermann and themselves were Konrad von Kardoroff, Hans Purrman, and Karl Scheffler, an art critic and Academy member, who eulogized Liebermann's greatness and humanity. The controlled press and radio of Nazi Germany made no mention of the event. Word nevertheless filtered through to the world outside. Scheffler later was given an honorary degree by a university in Zürich. Those on the inside knew it was a tribute to his moral courage even more than to his art criticism.

During 1936 a tormenting episode involved Käthe Kollwitz directly with the Nazi terror. She was interviewed by a foreign journalist who was gathering data on the way well-known artists were faring under Hitler. Her friend Otto Nagel was also present. Later the Russian newspaper *Izvestia* published an article on the interview, including the sentence, "We sat three together, talked about Hitler and the Third Reich, and looked each other deep in the eyes."

On July 13 two Gestapo officers entered the Kollwitz home and threatened the artist with concentration camp. They assured her that neither her age—then sixty-nine—nor anything else would protect her. Next day, in a follow-up action, one of them came to her studio, examined her work, and finally asked her to write a statement for the press repudiating the *Izvestia* article. This she did, including also a declaration that in talking to the journalist she had contradicted his statements about Russia. Despite her great

"Self-portrait with Hand on Brow" (*Selbstbildnis*) Lithograph, 1934.
Staatliche Museen zu Berlin.

127

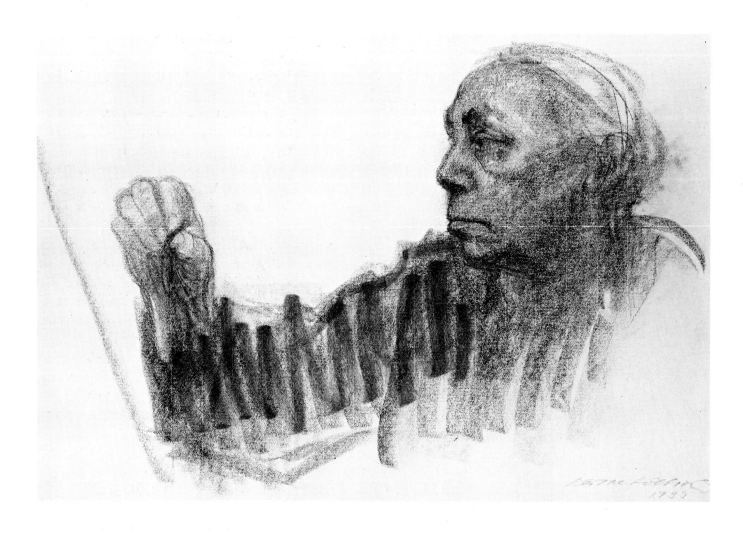

personal courage and self-respect, she had not felt that she could openly defy the Gestapo. She must have known all too well what had happened to those few who had dared to attempt this.

Days of worry and depression followed. Would the Gestapo be satisfied now and let her alone? Would there be more probing, perhaps even arrest and a concentration camp? She and Karl took counsel together. They decided that if a concentration camp seemed inevitable, they would both commit suicide. But first they would inform the Gestapo of their decision; this might help prevent such a fate.

Otto Nagel wrote later that during this time the artist arranged to meet him secretly. She warned him that the Gestapo had tried to force from her the name of the third person at that interview. But she assured him, "I did not tell them . . . and I will not . . ." She showed him a tiny flask, which she took from her blouse pocket, saying it was always with her. It was poison, her antidote for the terror of the Nazis.

She and Karl, however, escaped arrest and incarceration, though they truly could have said that all Germany had become a vast prison.

The artist was aware of the far greater terror and tragedy visited on many friends and acquaintances. To a Jewish friend she once wrote, "You are experiencing everything in your own body and soul. I experience it only through [my] friends." But even that indirect contact ". . . has often darkened my life."

In roundabout, even secret ways artists not in favor of the regime managed sometimes to show mutual solidarity and support. During that July of 1936 Käthe Kollwitz learned with joy that she would receive 1,500 marks to be used in converting her "Protecting Mother" sculpture from plaster to stone. The donor was another Secession artist, the excellent portrait painter Leo von Koenig, son of a German general and maker of some revealing likenesses of Nazi leaders. He had raised the money by selling some land to the House of Krupp, the munitionmakers who were now working at top speed to supply Hitler's new armies with tools for the coming destruction. The artist hoped that she might eventually repay her friend von Koenig by selling some pieces of her own art work.

The Academy of Arts was preparing for autumn 1936 an historic exhibition honoring 150 years of sculpture in Berlin. Käthe Kollwitz hoped that some of her own work might be included. Around Easter of that year she talked about it with a friendly museum head, Eberhard Hanfstaengl, who advised her that there was opposition in high places to the inclusion of her works.

He showed her his sympathy, however, by allowing her to enter a closed room in the basement which contained works of art that the Nazis had already ordered removed from public view. There for the first time she saw the original of Ernst Barlach's haunting "War Memorial," a wood sculpture which had been removed from the Magdeburg Cathedral in 1934, early in the Hitler era.

She gazed long at the six contrasting figures that Barlach had grouped around a graveyard cross—an unmistakable indictment of war. Later in her diary she noted her own approval, even though this work was ". . . impossible, naturally, for supporters of the Third Reich." But nonetheless it was true for her and many others. Then she mentioned the fact that the face of the mother figure was hidden by a shawl, and added the admiring notation "Good, Barlach!"

Two of her sculptures were actually chosen for inclusion in that autumn Academy exhibition. One was the original plaster of the mother figure from the "Mourning Parents," the other a poignant, small bronze relief plaque, which is today part of her tombstone in East Berlin. This she named "Rest in the Peace of His Hands," from the Goethe quotation which inspired it. These two works were part of the exhibition to which she was allowed a preview look before it opened for the general public.

Elation filled her that her work was thus included. She told her friend Jeep that "vibrating together" was, after all, "beautiful and alive," for ". . . it is sad to be excluded. One is but a leaf on a twig, and the twig belongs to the whole tree, and when the tree sways back and forth, the leaf is content to sway with it."

However, it was the dictators of Germany who determined how the tree swayed. They decided that this leaf was to be cut off. Suddenly, the day before the exhibition opened, her two pieces were removed. So too were

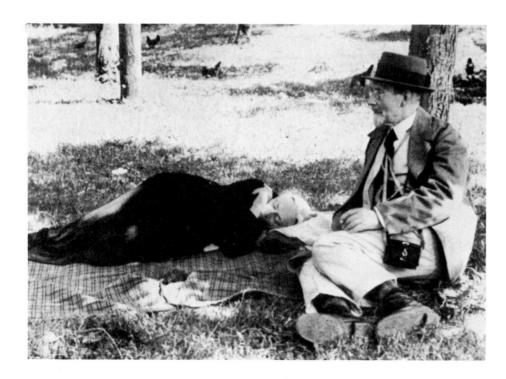

Käthe and Karl Kollwitz resting in the outdoors, 1935.

four sculptures by Barlach as well as other works. All were apparently to be stored out of sight in a room reserved for junk. But amidst confusions not uncommon in that period, her pieces reappeared for the time being in the soon-to-be-closed museum, the Crown Prince Palace.

The artist, however, knew that now the knell had rung for her public artistic activity in Germany. She feared even that Nazi influence might reach into Belgium and cause the removal of the "Mourning Parents" from the cemetery where her son Peter was buried. Her temporary intoxication at being allowed to sway with other leaves on the national tree now gave way to grim stoicism. She wrote, "Everything must be lived through . . ."

Before 1936 ended further notorious decrees were issued. They laid the foundations for the purging—actual removal and seizure—from museums and other collections of art works considered degenerate by Hitler, Goebbels, Goering, Rust, and their sycophants, who step by step had taken almost unlimited control over art, artists, art criticism, and art viewers.

The Nazi party's central newspaper, *Völkischer Beobachter*, printed a sneering comment on the "Mourning Mother," which so closely resembled the artist herself: "Thank God a German mother does not look like this." Yet even much later bits and pieces of approval were not entirely absent. As late as 1942 Hans Weigert's history of German art, though it made no mention of Kollwitz graphics, did reproduce that same "Mourning Mother," praising it as ". . . the latest and most powerful German 'Pietà.'" Consistency was not a characteristic of the Hitler era.

The artist herself tried to digest the grim reality. She noted in November 1936, "I have really come to the end of my work." She mentioned vague plans for a small sculpture and a relief. But to what end? Do them or not, it made no difference—". . . not for others, and also not for me."

The silence of others—all the cowed and conforming crowd—thundered in her mind. After her works had been removed, first from the Academy sculpture exhibit, then later from the museum in the Crown Prince Palace, she had received almost no expressions of sympathy. She had thought people would visit her or at least write their regrets. But instead, "Such a stillness around me."

Nevertheless, "Karl is still here. Daily I see him and we talk and show each other that we love . . . . But how will it be when he too is gone?" There was no answer but silence.

In 1937 the Nazi steamroller flattened and degraded German art. In Munich, "mother" city of the Nazi movement, a grandiose House of German

Art had been built from plans personally supervised by Hitler. The Führer esteemed himself a genius in architecture as well as a gifted artist whose career had been thwarted by Jewish influences in Vienna years before the start of the First World War. In a violent seventy-minute speech at the opening of the new House of German Art, Hitler poured out hatred of modern art—decadent, Bolshevist, Jewish corruption. There was no room for it in his Third Reich, which was to endure for a thousand years. Art works not understandable to the average German would be eliminated. As for modern artists, if they painted as they did because they saw things that way, then they " . . . should be dealt with in the Ministry of the Interior, where sterilization of the insane is arranged." But if they did not see things that way and yet persisted in painting so, they "should be dealt with by the criminal courts."

In the spacious House of German Art were displayed more than eight hundred paintings, drawings, and sculptures that were pleasing to Hitler's taste and made by approved German artists, mostly since the Nazi takeover in 1933. Hardly a single piece rose above the level of mediocrity. Not one had a vestige of antiwar content. Many glorified combat and the military way of life. The day after the opening of the House of German Art the Nazi dictators opened in an old gallery a "degenerate art" display, supposed to be a kind of chamber of horrors, disgusting to all true Germans. Here were crowded more than seven hundred works by one hundred artists from the period 1918 to 1933.

They were jammed into sections labeled MOCKERY OF CHRISTIANITY, DEFILEMENT OF GERMAN WOMANHOOD, SLANDER OF GERMAN HEROES (the antiwar art), JEWISH ART, and so on. To underscore the message a printed guide was supplied, complete with quotations from Hitler. No Kollwitz work was included either here or in the approved House of German Art. She was simply disregarded.

The "degenerate" exhibit proved an unexpected rival to the House of German Art. The New York *Herald-Tribune* reported that ". . . it was far more popular . . . than the exhibition of Nazi art. Thousands of persons, mainly art students or those with cultivated tastes, crowded the three large halls of the old gallery to enjoy the pictures condemned by the Nazis."

Between mid-July and November 1937 more than two million visitors saw the "degenerate" show in Munich. Early in 1938 it moved on to other German cities: Berlin, Leipzig, Düsseldorf, Frankfurt, Cologne. In Britain, anti-Hitler art lovers staged a counter-exhibition at the Burlington Gallery to expose the Nazi control over art and culture.

During February 1937 Käthe Kollwitz found new evidence that the Nazis had condemned her to oblivion. Though plans had been made to show some of her works at the Nierendorff Galleries in Berlin, these plans simply vanished like water evaporating in the hot sun. "Always the same reason," she noted.

But signs of life reached her from outside Germany a few months later. An exhibition of her works had been held in New York City, and a Jewish woman artist—an émigré from Germany—sent her a review of it.

Käthe Kollwitz replied with thanks, expressing happiness that at least in the United States her works were being shown. How depressing, she wrote, to be treated like one of the nonliving in her own country! She mentioned her recent work, almost solely in sculpture. The "Protecting Mother" was completed. She planned now to do only small things. She hoped, for autumn of 1937, to have a large exhibition in "northern lands" (Scandinavia).

An association of Danish artists wanted to exhibit some of her graphic works. Indeed, a Danish cabinet minister named Zahle offered to take her prints from Germany to Denmark himself. But permission was refused by Goebbels' Ministry of Propaganda and Enlightenment, now in full control of artistic matters. Later a children's home in Norway sought to buy the "Protecting Mother," but the Nazi regime refused to issue the required export permit.

The repression was more complete than she had first expected, for in 1933, when the Nazi era had just begun, she had expressed the thought that by the time of her seventieth birthday in 1937 she would be allowed to exhibit in Germany—or at least outside Germany.

That birthday drew near, and the Buchholz Bookshop and Gallery on Leipziger Street, Berlin, did plan a small Kollwitz showing for the occasion —but it was forbidden. The artist voiced her mingled anger and despair in letters to two friends, Marie Baum and the well-known writer Ricarda Huch. The ban on the exhibit had been no surprise, for the artist knew what had happened in Munich—and had reacted to it with both laughter and anger. However, these reactions were futile, private satisfactions rather than useful ones. "One can't change things." Hence, "one's fists remain in one's pockets."

Yet—according to the writer Lenka von Koerber—some of the artist's friends did manage to see her works despite the ban. In the downstairs book section of the Buchholz shop a curtained door opened on a stairway to the tiny art gallery above. If someone came into the shop asking for the Kollwitz exhibit, he was told that unfortunately it had been closed—but the artwork was still upstairs in the gallery. Silently, one by one, the visitors approached the drapes, moved them aside, climbed the small stairway, and looked at the works of their great blacklisted friend, including the "Protecting Mother."

One of the other artists who worked at the Kloster Street studio building wrote of Käthe Kollwitz in this period. She appeared old, stooped, very quiet, but magnetic, and with a great motherliness. Irresistibly, "One had to love her. In this period of oppression, she who had been persecuted and insulted gave comfort and hope to us younger ones."

The best of the artistic and intellectual creativity of Germany had been silenced within the country or driven into exile outside it. More and more the audience for Kollwitz was to be found beyond the borders of the war-oriented Hitler Reich. In June 1937 one significant showing of her work took place in a distant city—at the Zeitlin Gallery and Bookshop in Los Angeles. It was opened with spoken tributes to the great and aged artist by Ernst Toller, a refugee dramatist from Germany, and by the composer George Antheil.

In an article published at that time one of the authors of this book called her "... Germany's greatest artist, for who today remaining in the ... Reich can be named to compare with her?" Her art was described in that article as "... representative of the best in the culture of the real 'German people'— a people truly of poets and thinkers, not of Nazi hijackers, military warlords, and armament barons."

Although her work was suppressed in her own country, "she cannot be silenced . . . for her matchless prints . . . and drawings live in the eyes and minds of a faithful army of enthusiasts the world over. Their silent intensity outshouts the massed loudspeakers of the charlatans and mountebanks who have taken over the rule of Germany for a time." A concluding prediction was ventured: "In a Germany freed, the art of Kollwitz will again be disseminated among the masses of people, of and for whom her work is done. . . ."

For health reasons the artist herself went with her husband, shortly before her seventieth birthday in 1937, to Bad Reinerz, a spa near Glatz in Silesia (now part of Poland). She was overwhelmed to receive some 150 letters and telegrams of congratulations on her birthday.

Also, she had received a letter from Jake Zeitlin telling of the successful showing of her work at his gallery and elsewhere and expressing the desire to handle more of her prints in the future. She mentioned this good news when, on July fifth, just three days before her birthday, she wrote to a friendly art dealer in Berlin. In her flowing script she told him of the final certainty she felt: for her, there was nothing more to hope for in Germany. Hence it was necessary to look to other lands as outlets for her work—"above all probably to America." Late that month she wrote in another letter, "For Germany I am dead, but for America I have begun to come alive. That is wonderful!"

Also, she counted her blessings: she still had her husband after almost forty-seven years of marriage; she had four grandchildren; and her son Hans's entire family in Lichtenrade was a source of joy and comfort.

The oppression in Germany still grew. In August 1937 Goering issued an historic decree ordering immediate action to rid all Germany's museums and galleries of art works considered degenerate or unsuitable by the Führer and his sub-Führers. This purge was to be carried on ". . . without regard to legal forms or property relationships." Goering reserved for himself the decision as to final disposition of the state-owned works thus removed.

The resulting purge was executed in more than one hundred German museums. Prints and drawings by Käthe Kollwitz were among some 12,000 graphic works and 5,000 paintings that disappeared during this huge action. The Nazis conducted a profitable business, selling prints by Kollwitz and many others through Switzerland. Some museum officials managed, however, to hide away Kollwitz items in the hope of better times.

Goering confiscated for himself more than a dozen extremely valuable "degenerate" paintings. Later, as the Nazi armies overran much of Europe, he added other unpaid-for treasures to his enormous private hoard.

Käthe Kollwitz revealed impressive reserves of fortitude and notable self-control. She was neither ignorant of the terrible realities nor rash in facing them. She even managed to look beyond some oddly outrageous incidents in which Nazi editors pirated her works. Early in 1938 a pro-fascist magazine printed in both Italian and German published all seven prints from a series that had become known as her *Hunger* portfolio. They were credited, however, only to ". . . an important German artist." No name was given. She had made them fourteen years before for the International Workers

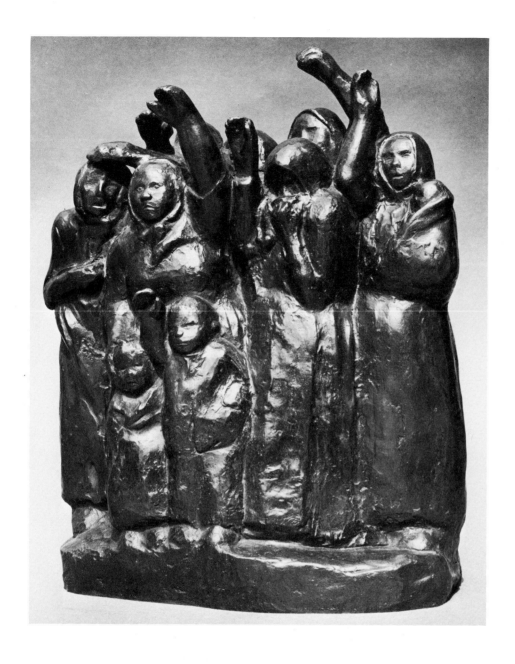

"Soldiers' Wives Waving Good-by" (*Abschiedwinkende Soldatenfrauen*) Bronze, 1937.

This compact group, showing seven women and three or more children, has an actual size of no more than about 9¾ inches wide and 12⅞ inches high. German women, within a relatively few months after this was made, were actually waving good-by to their men, off to fight, first in Spain, then all over Europe.
Photograph by courtesy of Marlborough Fine Art (London) Ltd.

Aid. Now they were presented as pictures of "Hunger in the Red Paradise."

Another time, her lithograph "Bread!" from that same portfolio was given the signature of a "Herr Frank" and used by a Nazi magazine for women to illustrate pro-fascist verses in both German and Spanish. The lithograph was thus twisted to seem to apply to Spain. Both Hitler and Mussolini, the fascist dictator of Italy, had sent soldiers and bombers to help General Franco's revolt against the Spanish Republic, which—abandoned by the democracies of Europe and the United States—finally fell early in 1939,

"Self-portrait in Profile, Facing Right" (*Selbstbildnis im Profil nach Rechts*) Lithograph, 1938. The lithographic stone has in this case been preserved. The original here was about 18¾ × 11¼ inches. *Kunsthalle, Hamburg.*

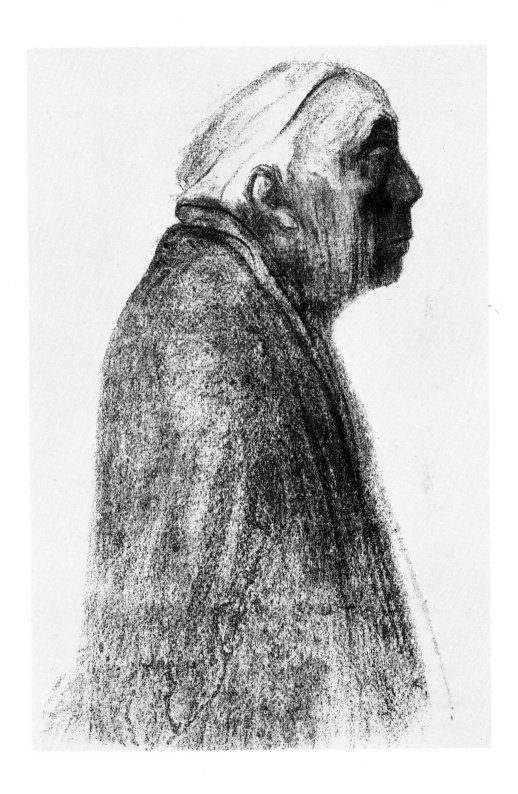

having served as a dress rehearsal for the Second World War which broke out before the end of the year.

Käthe Kollwitz called these thefts of her art more amusing than annoying. She preferred not to protest, for if she did and were named as the real artist, it would seem she willingly aided fascism in Spain and elsewhere. But if she replied that she wanted no part of *that*, she would be considered actively pro-Communist with all the dangers this involved in Germany.

His formidable war machine now ready for action, Hitler continued the aggressions that had always been his aim. In September 1938 when the British and French governments sacrificed the Czechoslovak democracy to Hitler's demands, Käthe Kollwitz, voicing her perpetual dread of war, wrote in her diary, "War has been avoided! Thank you, Chamberlain." Someone in the British Parliament had said there was nothing in the world important enough to justify plunging the nations into another world war. Least of all, she added ironically, could war be justified by the sentiment *Deutschland über alles* (Germany above all).

The betrayal of Czechoslovakia and other concessions by the European powers merely enabled Hitler to move ahead his timetable for war, which he intended should make his Reich dominant in Europe. These ruthless aims were served by the anti-Semitism, the internal terror, and the other outrages that Käthe Kollwitz deplored, even when she could not grasp all the cynical motives behind them. Near the end of 1938 she wrote to a Jewish woman who was later able to leave Germany, "Believe me, we all suffer deeply together. Pain and shame we feel. And indignation." Later she completed a relief memorial showing four clasped hands for the gravestone of this woman's husband in the Jewish cemetery of Cologne.

Käthe Kollwitz did on at least one occasion voice her indignation and sense of outrage in the heart of her family. In the Nazi-controlled schools the children of Hans and Ottilie Kollwitz heard endless repetitions of praise for the Führer. They repeated in their grandmother's presence some of this political education. Kollwitz could not stand to listen and flared up: "*Der Hitler,*" she burst out, "*ist ein Esel!*" (Hitler is an ass!)

Fortunately her grandchildren were not the sort to repeat such a rash outburst to outsiders. In many another German family a careless or hasty comment by elders was reported by indoctrinated children—with terrifying consequences.

The fascist terror, pervasive, ruthless, and unremitting, worked like a poison through all Germany. In rural Güstrow, a village in the province of

"Barlach in Death" (*Barlach auf dem Totenbett*) Charcoal drawing, October 27, 1938, done following the artist's return from the funeral services for Barlach.
Deutsche Fotothek Dresden.

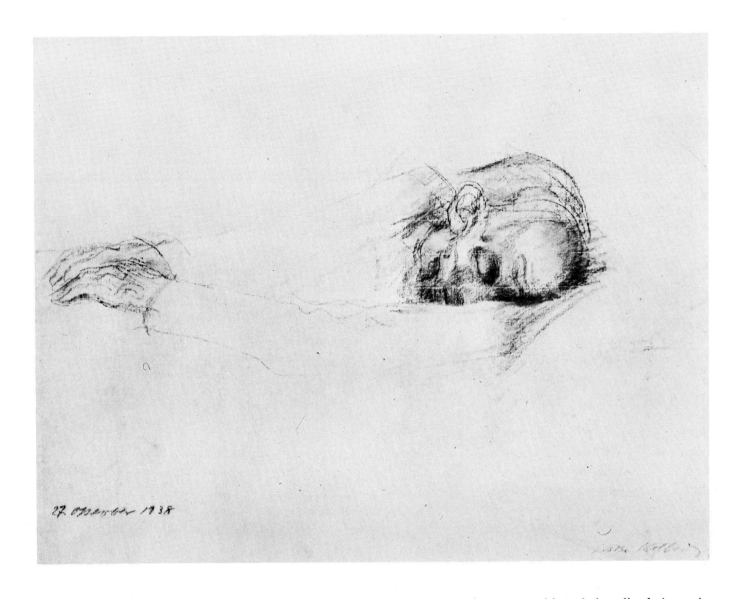

27. October 1938

Mecklenburg, isolation and persecution were taking their toll of the artist Ernst Barlach, as they had of Max Liebermann in Berlin, and so many other artists. Käthe Kollwitz, who felt herself bound to Barlach in many subtle ways, was full of compassion. What Barlach experienced, she told a friend, was doubly hard. She herself had her husband, ". . . with whom I can always talk, and who is always close. . . . Barlach has no one."

Barlach died on October 24, 1938, at the age of sixty-eight. His few remaining friends could not doubt that but for the ostracism he had suffered he would have lived longer and produced more great work. Käthe Kollwitz traveled to Güstrow for the memorial service. As she had done with the murdered Liebknecht, she sketched Barlach—one of her greatest drawings. He looked so small, so sunken into himself, his head turned to one side as if to

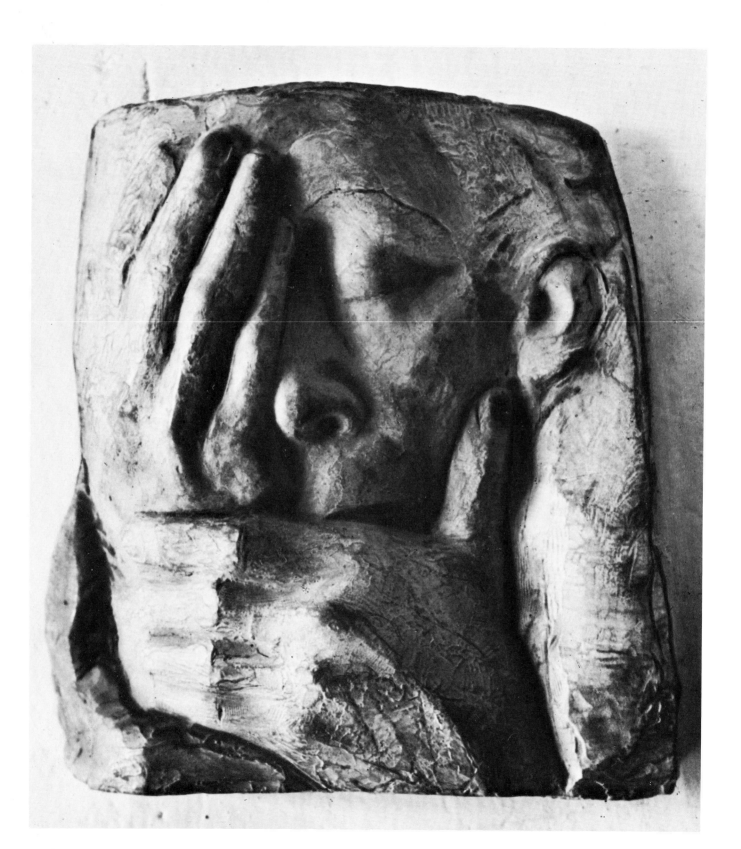

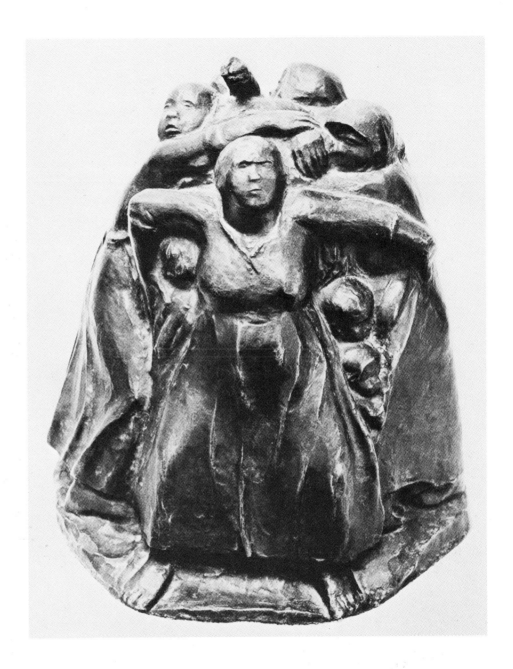

reject the life in which he had been rejected, despite all he had given to his fellowmen.

At the Barlach memorial service she was again one of a tiny number who braved Nazi displeasure to honor the dead. With her were the painter Leo von Koenig and the sculptor Gerhard Marcks. Over Barlach's coffin hung the mask he had made of the "Hovering Angel," with a face like that of a younger Käthe Kollwitz.

The fate of the bronze original of that figure was symbolic. Seized by the

were poured flaming into a final great lithograph, which was completed in 1942. An old woman, dour and defiant, is like an angry bird protecting her young in their nest. The woman is beyond doubt Käthe Kollwitz herself. The artist's own comment underscored the militance of the print. The children she had drawn she called "real Berlin youngsters." They are ". . . like horses, eagerly scenting the outdoors."

Those children are, as her own son and grandson, the two Peters, had been, fair prey for the warmakers. But this old woman of the lithograph will not allow them to be taken. She has ". . . stuck the youngsters under her. . . . Powerfully and commandingly she spread her arms and hands. . . . 'Seed for the planting shall not be ground up!'" This outcry seems to echo another, "Never again war!"

This print is, in short, ". . . not a longed-for wish, but a demand, a command!" To Jeep she added also that the mother figure tells the boys, ". . . when you are grown you must adjust to life, but never again to war." This great graphic command came from her heart.

One day in October 1942 her son Hans came quietly into her room. She knew without a word that her beloved grandson, Peter, had been killed. It had happened on September 22nd in Russia. Like his uncle, the Peter slain twenty-eight years earlier, he had been sacrificed—and for what?

Old Käthe—as she often called herself now—tried to be strong, to comfort the boy's parents and his surviving sisters and brother. But the new blow struck her where she had few defenses.

The war went badly, despite the claims of Nazi propaganda. American as well as British bombers now increased their raids on Berlin and other major German population and industrial centers. Nights and days, too, the artist, like millions of others around her, heard the air-raid warnings scream and took to shelters. It became harder and harder for her to get to safety even with help.

Amidst it all, she managed to think of others beside herself and her immediate family. As late as May 1943 she tried to give practical help to victims of the ever-increasing drive to persecute and exterminate Jews, or semi-Jews. Her sister Lise's husband, Georg Stern (who had died in 1934), had been Jewish, though thoroughly Germanized in outlook and interests. His brother, too, had married a non-Jewish woman. That brother's daughter, Klara, was in 1943 the artist's companion and dear friend. Nazi laws allowed Klara's "mixed" parents to rent living quarters only from full Jews or from other "hybrids." They were about to lose their present lodgings and could

"Seed for the Planting Shall Not Be Ground Up" (*Saatfrüchte sollen nicht vermahlen werden*) Lithograph, 1942.

The size of the original is about 14⅝ × 15½ inches. The lithographic stone has been destroyed. Relatively few prints are known to have been made of this, the artist's last lithograph. Most of them are signed by the artist. The one reproduced here has, in addition to the signature, her dedication to her lifelong friend, Beate Bonus-Jeep. The inscription reads: "To dear Jeep from her old Schmidt, 1942." *Staatliche Museen zu Berlin.*

find nothing else in Berlin, which was beginning to suffer serious housing shortages because of the constant bombings.

On their behalf old Käthe wrote to acquaintances who might have space that could be used by these "very fine, very cultivated" people, the Sterns. Even so small a gesture of humanity was rare in that place and time. It had been almost two years earlier when Goering issued the notorious order to make preparations for the ". . . total solution of the Jewish question in the German-controlled areas of Europe." That solution became the systematic

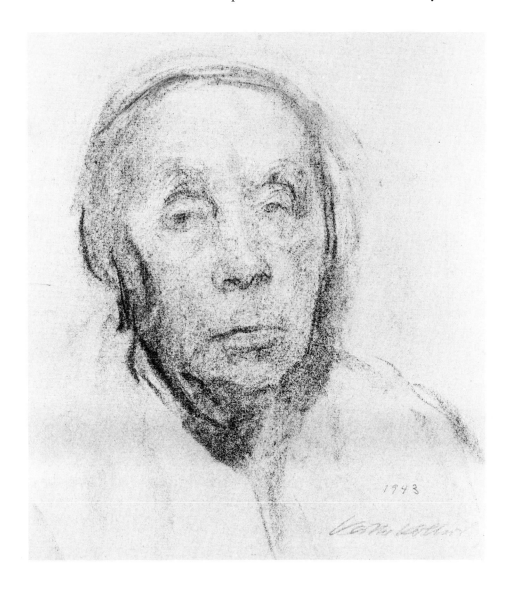

1943

"Self-portrait" (*Selbstbildnis*)
Charcoal drawing, 1943.
Very likely the last of the many self-portraits by the artist. The signature at lower right is hers, but the date has been added by another hand.
Kunsthalle, Hamburg.

degradation and slaughter of five to six million Jews of all ages, together with other ethnic minorities—mass genocide.

The final entry in the diaries of Käthe Kollwitz is dated May 1943. It records a precious visit to Hans and his family at Lichtenrade to celebrate his fifty-first birthday. The night of May fourteenth brought air-raid alarms, yet the Kollwitzes, sitting late in the garden listening to a nightingale, had managed to drink in some beauty also. There was the comfort of being with Hans, Ottilie, and Lise.

She gave Hans as birthday gifts some art works of special meaning to them both: the relief sculpture she had made for their family grave, a drawing of Karl reading aloud, and the tender little etching "Greeting," on which she had been working when Hans was about to be born. This visit marked a finale for the family.

Air raids on Berlin became more devastating until by the war's end about half its housing had been destroyed, although two-thirds of its many factories managed to work on, supplying the hopeless effort to avert defeat. To her daughter-in-law, Ottilie, Käthe said that later on, in the future, people would ". . . hardly be able to understand this period." Somehow she still managed to think of a future that was different from this nightmarish present.

By mid-1943 it was clear that in order to survive old Käthe should no longer be allowed to risk remaining in the place where she had lived and worked for more than fifty years.

A refuge was found. Margaret Böning, a devoted young sculptor, lived at Nordhausen in the Harz region about 120 miles southeast of Berlin. She offered to share her house with Käthe Kollwitz, whom she deeply admired as an artist and woman. Reluctantly old Käthe left her own longtime home. With her to Nordhausen went her widowed sister, Lise; Lise's daughter, Katta Stern, a dancer; and Lise's niece, Klara.

May had not ended when Käthe wrote to Hans and his family. She was sitting on a lovely balcony at Nordhausen and had been repeating to herself from memory sections of Goethe's *Faust*. She urged her children not to worry about her. If air raids should come to Nordhausen, too, she promised to take refuge promptly in the cellar.

Writing, or dictating to Klara, she managed to correspond with family and friends. She sent a plea to Otto Nagel, his wife, and infant daughter to carry on somehow in spite of the mounting destruction. "Forward now. Life will somehow take care of things. Toward a better future."

All too soon it became clear that that future could not include return to her Berlin home and work place. The air raids intensified, and the tide of war in Russia went more and more against the Nazi armies. With the help of Klara, who lived when she could in the Kollwitz apartment on Weissenburger Street, many of the artist's drawings were removed for safety. One portfolio went to the Prince of Saxony, an avid art collector with an ancestral residence at Moritzburg near Dresden. The prince cherished her work and admired her both as an artist and woman.

Amidst his medical duties Hans Kollwitz managed to arrange safe shelter for his mother's massive statue "Protecting Mother." As a loan gift it went underground in the basement of the Crown Prince Palace, where once she had studied and admired the great antiwar memorial by Barlach.

On November 23, 1943, a great air raid blasted and burned out the entire building at 25 Weissenburger Street. Klara, injured, was unable to save the many pieces of art work still remaining there, including prints, plates, and even early paintings. Less than two weeks later the house of the Hans Kollwitz family at Lichtenrade was also destroyed in an air raid.

The artist at Nordhausen seemed quite crushed by these events. By early January 1944 she was confined to bed, her heart behaving badly. Her mood was blacker than her darkest woodcuts. She seemed devoid of any will to live. Yet during this dark period something took place almost too improbable to believe. A query came to her from an inquisitive stranger. He represented himself as a writer, gathering for a book the views of 100 well-known artists on what constituted honor and worth in art. His request to her included the insulting implication, typical of the Nazi era, that her own work had been "gutter art"—ugly, not genuine art.

Today it seems likely that the whole thing was a scheme this man had concocted to secure autographs on letters from well-known personalities in the art world, rather than genuine research for a planned book or article. However, old Käthe could know nothing of that.

She laughed over the impudence of the letter, but it stirred her to reply. From the depths she roused herself and flung back at this voice of the Nazi present an answer as burning, bold, and defiant as her last lithograph. In this answer she summarized in a memorable way the whole of her life and aims.

An artist, she wrote, is above all a child of his period—especially when, as in her case, it was the period of the early socialist movement. It "... totally possessed me," she recalled. She had not, at first, tried consciously to serve the proletariat, but only to put into her art what she felt to be truly beautiful.

"Soldiers' Women" (*Soldatenfrauen*) Drawing in crayon, 1943. *Deutsche Fotothek Dresden.*

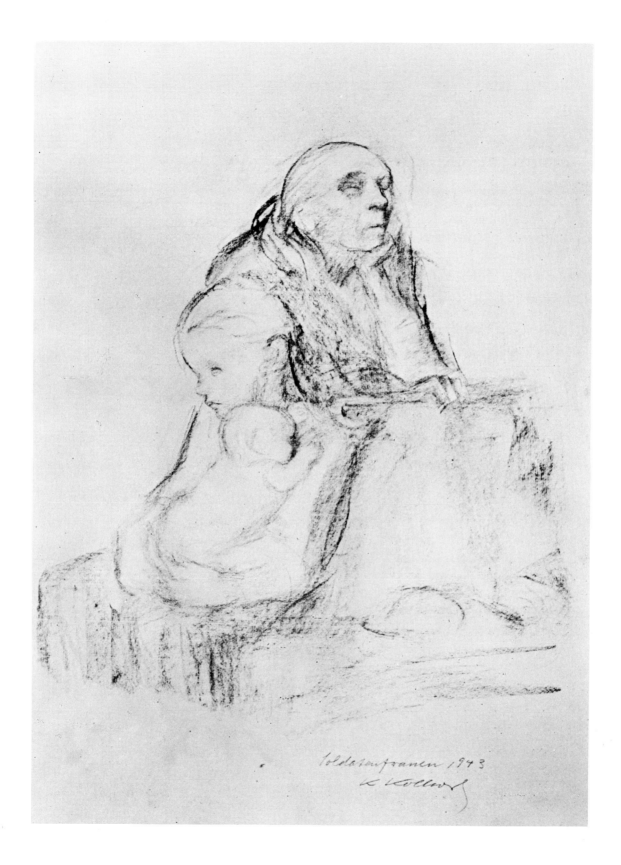

Soldatenfrauen 1943
K Kollwitz

The only laws of beauty that meant anything to her were those she herself perceived and felt. They did not include those of the Greeks. "What did I care about them?"

"For me," she went on, "the proletariat was beautiful. The outward appearance of typical workers stimulated me to portray them. Only later when, through closer contact, I really learned to know the misery and poverty of the workers did there arise [in me] a feeling of obligation—to serve them by means of my art."

In a final gesture of dignity and integrity she told her prying questioner that it mattered not a bit to her whether he did or did not include her among his 100 celebrities. But if he did wish to use her reply, he must use it in full or not at all. And in conclusion: "I stand by every piece of work that I have issued; of each of them I have demanded that it be good."

Early in June 1944 she confessed, "I feel myself very old and done for, and hope my life doesn't last much longer." Yet even then her companions at Nordhausen noted her interest and pleasure in the conversation of the younger women around her. As before, the nearness of youth nourished and revived her. Her own seventy-seventh birthday on July 8, 1944, brought visits from her daughter-in-law Ottilie and her old friend Jeep.

More and more the artist seemed to attain a sort of stoic peace. Bridges to the past had been all but bombed away. "One gets a complete housecleaning," she observed wryly. "I give no thought to the future. There's no sense in doing so." Yet her own personality did not dull or disintegrate.

A Danish woman, Helga Kaae, traveled illegally all the way to Nordhausen to bring her news that her foster son, Georg Gretor, had died. The visitor found her indeed "a very old woman," but one whose presence radiated something inescapably impressive.

Even Nordhausen seemed unsafe as the war went more and more against Hitler. He had made hysterical, wasteful efforts to terrorize the British population centers with aerial weapons of revenge—first the V–1 buzz bombs then the V–2 rockets created by Wernher von Braun and others. Even greater increases in the Anglo-American bombings of German cities and towns were expected by way of counterreprisal. Berlin announced plans to quarter elderly refugees, such as Käthe Kollwitz, among peasants living in remote rural regions.

Such a move could have meant intolerable hardships for the ailing, failing artist. So, at least, it seemed to one aristocratic and attentive admirer and art collector—Prince Ernst Heinrich of Saxony. He wanted to assist her, and also to enlarge his family collection of fine prints and drawings.

"Since no help was offered to her," he recalled a couple of years later, "I invited her to come to Moritzburg." There at his family's ancestral seat, he ". . . tried to make her life as pleasant as possible . . . ," regarding this as ". . . an obligation . . . to this great, unique German artist."

At about the same time in 1944 the American periodical *Art Digest*, reviewing an exhibition of Kollwitz works at the Galerie St. Etienne in New York City, noted with concern, "No word has been received from Frau Kollwitz since 1941 . . . and the current exhibit may contain a portion of the last work she was allowed to do."

The artist's final move was made late in 1944. Old Käthe and her granddaughter Jutta took up modest quarters in the Rudenhof, an auxiliary building of Moritzburg, about 120 miles east of Nordhausen. In her simple room at the Rudenhof she had copies of some books by Goethe, and Goethe's mask hung over her narrow bed, where she could feel it even when she could not see it.

Jutta brought her drawing materials from nearby Dresden, long a leading center of art and architecture in Saxony. But old Käthe drew no more. Her eyes were failing, and she could not bear to make anything that fell short of the works of her past—the works she still stood by and knew to be good, despite the Nazi dictators.

The horror came close even here. On February 14, 1945, nearby Dresden was ravaged by Allied bombers in the most stupendous and murderously destructive of all fire bombings. Moritzburg, however, escaped actual damage.

Though old Käthe weakened, she remained aware of the meaning of events in this war that would, all too obviously, outlast her. Soviet armies now advanced irresistibly from the east. People in Saxony around her, she noted, were privately beginning to anticipate and plan for a Russian-influenced future. In a letter to Hans and his family the artist suggested that Arne, her surviving grandson, should begin learning Russian. It would be an advantage because of the many relationships she foresaw that the future would bring between Germany and Russia.

In a letter of February 21, 1945, she spoke out clear and strong. Germany's cities were now heaps of rubble, she noted; but even worse was the fact that every war carried ". . . in its pocket . . ." another counter-war, a war of reprisal. War would be answered by war ". . . until everything is in

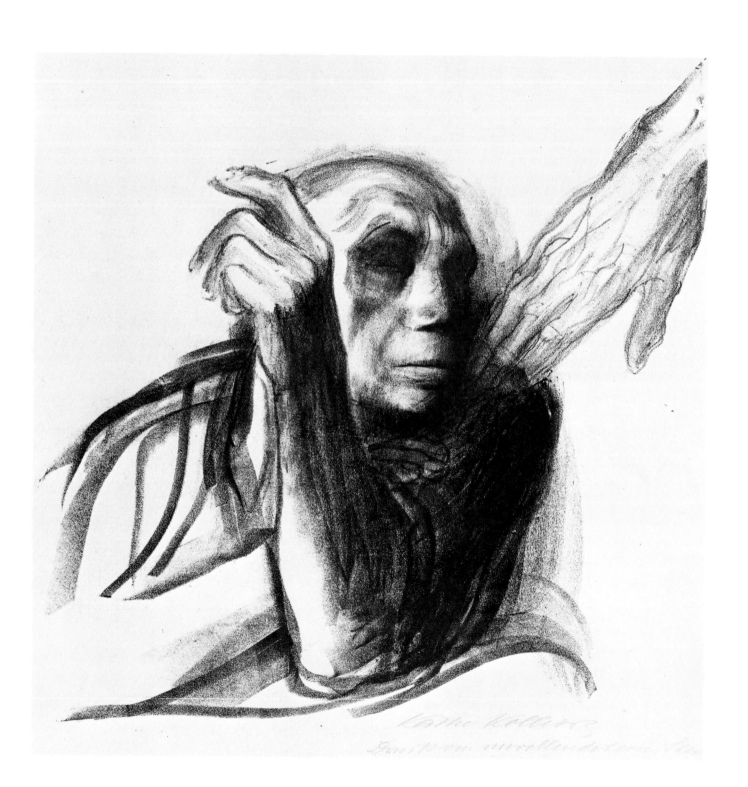

LEFT:
"The Call of Death" (*Ruf des Todes*) Lithograph, 1934–1935. "Death Summons" could be an alternate title for this, the eighth and final print in the series called *Death* (*Tod*). *Kunsthalle, Hamburg.*

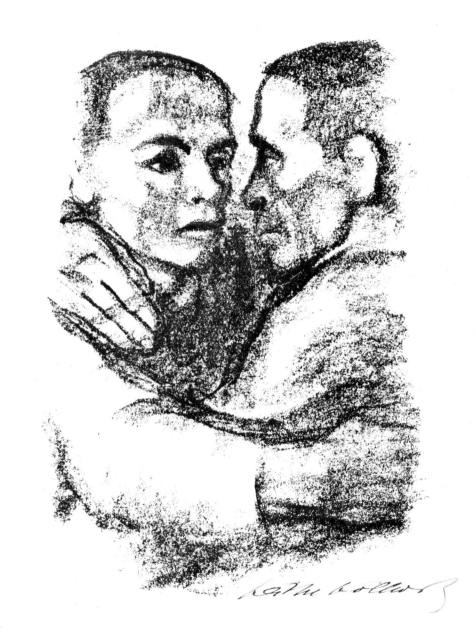

RIGHT:
"Fraternization of the Nations" (*Verbrüderung der Nationen*), also known as "Fraternity" (*Verbrüderung*) Lithograph, 1924.

This image originated as an illustration for a book by a French writer, Henri Barbusse, entitled *The Singing Soldier*. *Kupferstichkabinett, Dresden. Photograph taken by Deutsche Fotothek Dresden.*

ruins." And then, ". . . the devil only knows . . ." what would become of the world or of Germany.

She could see but one way out from this vista of unending horror and death. "With my whole heart I am for a radical end to all this insanity. Only from world-wide socialism do I expect anything."

She longed for one last visit from Hans and begged him by letter, almost pitifully, to come if he possibly could or to tell her if he could not; then she could die in peace, as she desired. In spite of terrible travel difficulties, Hans made a last visit to his mother in Moritzburg on Good Friday, 1945. He read aloud to her from the Easter story in the Gospel according to St. Matthew, which she had heard often in the mighty oratorio by Johann Sebastian Bach. He read, too, the scene of the Easter walk from the first part of Goethe's *Faust*. Hans took back with him a final image of his mother. Amidst all the destruction and decline she had seemed like a queen in exile, a monarch of unfailing goodness and dignity.

Her last letter, written April 16, 1945, showed awareness that death, which she had so often pictured, was drawing near. "The war accompanies me to the end," she wrote. How happy she would have been to see the war— all war—ended. But she knew that she would not live that long.

Even so, she looked ahead and beyond. Her hope or vision of the future was expressed fervently during a conversation with her granddaughter Jutta. Reflecting the tensions of the times, Jutta asked whether Käthe did not love Germany.

"Yes, I do love it very much," she answered, "but even more I love the new idea. Do you know what it says in the Book of Revelations? A new time shall come, 'a new heaven and a new earth.' And they *will* come, too."

Germany, she felt, had a mission—a mission of peace—and she referred to a poem by C. F. Meyer (1825–1898) entitled "Peace on Earth," which climaxes in the line "Peace, peace upon the Earth!"

"I die with this conviction," said the artist. "People will have to work hard, but they will attain it!"

When Jutta asked whether she was a pacifist, Käthe Kollwitz replied, "Yes, if you understand by pacifism more than just antiwar. It is a new idea— that of the brotherhood of man." Socialism now meant to her, above all else, this longed-for fraternity of all mankind.

It was a great assertion of faith by an old woman, a spirit lofty and still soaring, dying in a land degraded and defeated.

chapter 10
April 22, 1945, and afterward

"Then People Will Have Been Enriched by Me"

Death came at last but not with violence or surprise. The date was April 22, 1945, only a few days before the unconditional surrender of the land she had loved and chosen not to leave despite its evil time of debasement and destruction.

Her body was cremated at nearby Meissen and the ashes interred in the small cemetery at Moritzburg. Jutta and Jördis Kollwitz, her twin granddaughters, who had cared for her during the last days, were both present, with only a few Moritzburg residents.

She had lived fully and well earned the final rest. It climaxed a life that met Aristotle's requirement for tragic drama: ". . . serious, complete, and of a certain magnitude."

During the months after her death, much of Germany seemed to undergo complete collapse as well as unconditional surrender. All but a few major cities lay deep in rubble. Five million slave laborers crowded the defeated Reich, herded together by the Nazis from all over their once-great empire. The dead and dying glutted the many concentration and extermination centers, now exposed in their full horror.

The sick, the starved, fugitives, refugees, all jostled in a ghastly *Walpurgisnacht*, or Witches' Sabbath. But even worse was the moral and mental degradation. A dozen years of Nazi gangsterism and conquest had corrupted most of a great people while destroying scores of millions of human lives and uncounted human goods within, and, especially, outside Germany.

Many intellectuals and professionals who had not lifted a finger to sup-

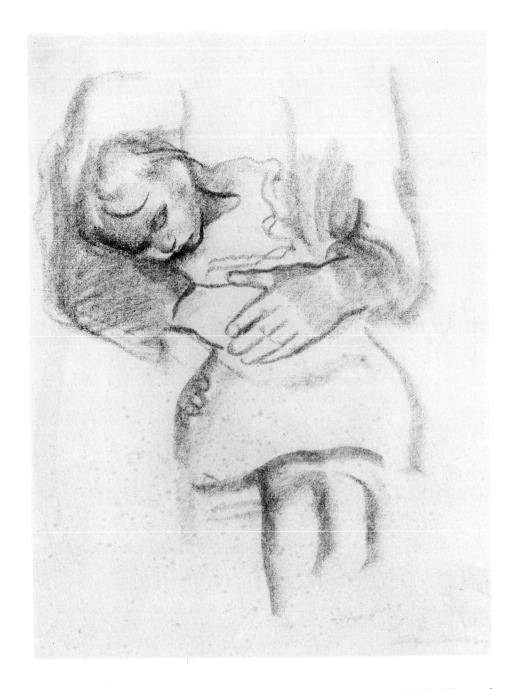

port Käthe Kollwitz during the years she was under the unpublished ban of the Nazis, now hastened to praise her work and courage, thus trimming their sails to the new winds. She herself—a realist and stoic, despite her vision of a finer future—might have smiled in irony at her rediscovery.

The era has been called a "zero point" in German history. Non-German observers might have found it strange that the artist herself had clung to the end to her high hopes for a better future. During the period of chaos, hunger, and breakdown, news of her death was slow to reach many of those closest to her and her art. Some of these, amid Berlin's rubble on July 8, 1945, recalled that this was the seventy-eighth anniversary of the birth of one of the few eminent residents of Germany who had not given in to the Nazi dictators.

Before August ended, however, definite word of her death at Moritzburg reached what was left of Berlin. The next month surviving members of her family were able to bring her ashes for burial beside those of her husband in the quiet central Friedrichsfelde cemetery (now part of East Berlin).

The Kollwitz family gravesite is marked by a simple slab bearing the unforgettable bronze relief that Käthe herself had created for this purpose in 1935–1936, a decade earlier. A sleeper with face like yet unlike that of the younger Käthe is securely ". . . resting in the peace of His hands," in the words of Goethe.

This image of unutterable and eternal peace continues a theme long close to her. It can be traced in a drawing made in 1900 as a study for the etching "Downtrodden Ones" (*Zertretene*); and it recurs in an undated drawing from much later—the sleeping child, secure in the arms of a protecting yet unseen mother. For to the artist they were a mother's hands, though Goethe had written "*His* hands."

Below this relief in simple letters are names and dates for the five family members interred there: her brother, Konrad Schmidt (1863–1932); her sister-in-law, Anna Schmidt (1867–1925); her brother-in-law, Georg Stern (1867–1934); her husband, Karl (1863–1940), to whose name is added the single identifying word *Arzt* (physician); and finally, the latest comer to this place of unbroken sleep:

KÄTHE KOLLWITZ (Born Schmidt)

Her much-loved sister, Lise Stern, was not buried there. She long outlived the artist, dying at the age of ninety-three after her mental powers had much declined. Arrangements could not be made by that time for her burial in East Berlin; she lies not far distant in a West Berlin cemetery.

Käthe Kollwitz was, in fact, the only one among the four—the three Schmidt daughters and the son Konrad—to whom old age did not bring senile decline. In her case a fine mind retained its powers and, indeed, seemed to gain new insights with age.

Today a more recent grave lies a few feet from the Kollwitz plot—that

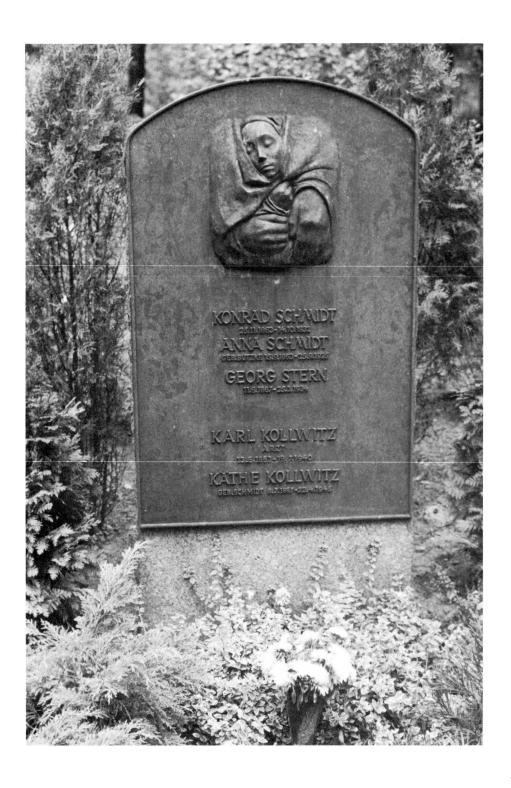

The Kollwitz gravesite with
the relief made by the artist a
decade before her death.
Photograph by H. A. Klein.

of Otto Nagel (1894–1967), the worker-artist, friend of both Käthe and Karl Kollwitz during their lives, who was buried so near at his own wish. After the war Nagel had become head of the Academy of Arts of the German Democratic Republic (East Germany) and wrote two books devoted to Kollwitz. His *Käthe Kollwitz*, a large, well-illustrated work, was first published in 1936 and in 1965, *The Self-Portraits of Käthe Kollwitz*.

Nagel also gathered an impressive number of photographic reproductions of the many superb drawings by Kollwitz in collections in Germany and elsewhere. He died before he could ready these for publication in a catalogue, but the work was carried forward by his daughter, Sybille Nagel Schallenberg. In 1969 an art historian, Dr. Werner Timm, began final preparation of this material for publication. The resulting catalogue, which is expected to appear before the middle of the decade of the 1970s, will be an illustrated guide to some 1,200 drawings made between 1888 and the early 1940s. Nagel and Timm are to be listed as coauthors when the work is published by the Henschel Press of East Berlin.

The German surrender in 1945 ended Hitler's Reich after a dozen years of deceit, aggression, destruction, and death. During the troubled era of postwar reconstruction, the banned works of Kollwitz began to reappear. They emerged from drawers, vaults, and hideaways where they had been secreted. Many, of course, were gone forever—lost because of the acts of the dictatorship that had ruled Germany or the bombs that had blasted it.

In July 1950 eighty-three years after Käthe's birth, a solemn ceremony took place in East Berlin on the spot where the building had stood in which the Kollwitzes lived and worked for more than half a century. The rubble of the great bombings had been cleared away and a small, pleasant park created. It bears the name Kollwitz Place and provides a pause in the length of Käthe Kollwitz Street, formerly Weissenburger Street.

Within the park on a stone pedestal is a large statue of old Käthe herself by the contemporary sculptor Gustav Seitz. There she sits, massive and solid in stone, her head thrust forward as it was in her last dark lithographed self-portrait. Her right hand in her lap holds a pencil; her left touches a portfolio of prints or drawings at her side. The statue seems heavy and literal, lacking the inner radiance, the dignity, the distinction that her living presence had revealed to so many who knew her. Yet the neighborhood children seem to find it a friendly sort of monument, for they clamber familiarly into the great stone lap. Käthe, who so loved children, might well have smiled, even

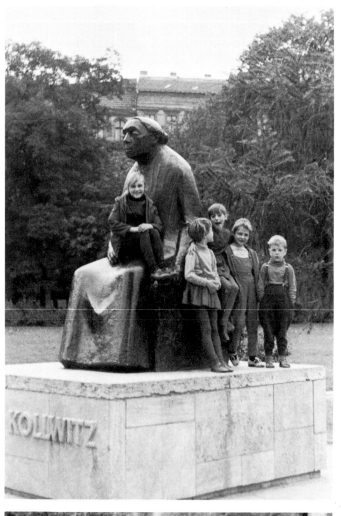

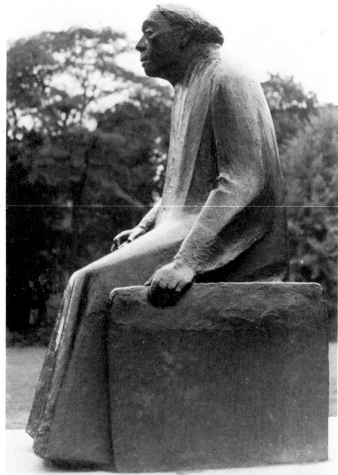

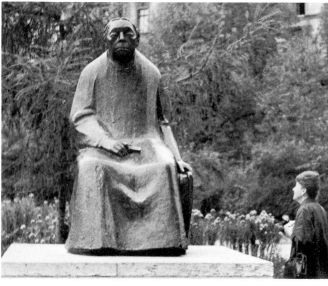

OPPOSITE:
The bronze statue of Käthe
Kollwitz attracts neighborhood
children, who play in this East
Berlin park, the Kollwitz Platz.
Photograph by H. A. Klein.

OPPOSITE LEFT:
Statue of Käthe Kollwitz by
Gustav Seitz in Kollwitz Place,
on the site in Berlin where she
lived for more than fifty years.
One of the authors studies the
monumental statue, showing
the artist with a drawing
instrument in her right hand,
and her left holding an artist's
portfolio.
Photograph by H. A. Klein.

OPPOSITE RIGHT:
The Kollwitz statue in the
park at Kollwitz Place, East
Berlin, seen from its left side.
The head thrust forward from
the neck is typical of the posture
of "old Käthe."
Photograph by H. A. Klein.

laughed aloud with the sudden exuberance she sometimes showed, had she
known that one day Berlin youngsters would play without awe on a stone
statue above the name KÄTHE KOLLWITZ.

The year 1955 brought publication of the definitive *Catalogue raisonné*
of her graphic works. Prepared by August Klipstein it details nearly 270
prints, dated 1890 to 1942—etchings, lithographs, woodcuts—in all their
known states and changes. It remains an essential tool of all Kollwitz study
and commentary.

In 1955 also a copy of her "Mourning Parents" was placed in a memorial
to the dead of both World Wars. It stands off a busy street in the Rhine-
side city of Cologne amidst ruins of a church destroyed in the Second World
War.

Between 1955 and 1957 the Roggevelde soldiers' cemetery where the
original "Mourning Parents" stood was moved to another Belgian site, also
near Diksmuide, West Flanders, at a place known as Vladsloo-Praebosch.
The two Kollwitz sculptures were moved together with the remains of the
fallen. Today, in silent but eloquent grief, both figures—the stone Käthe
and the stone Karl Kollwitz—brood not only over their second-born son,
Peter Kollwitz, and his comrades of World War I, but also over new
myriads of dead, for 26,000 are interred in this cemetery. Indeed the endless
vigil of these stone parents has come to commemorate all the millions of
victims of the enormous, bestial, and insane wars during the years since
1914. The Kollwitz statues constantly speak their unmistakable message to
the living. At the Vladsloo-Praebosch cemetery the visitors' book carried
this entry, dated September 22, 1966: "God bless you, Käthe. And all your
children. We carry on what you have wished." It is signed, "A former
enemy."

Many crowded years have passed since the artist's death. Steadily, even
swiftly, her work has gained recognition and become more popular in the
best sense of the word. Volumes many times the size of this could be filled
with details of her numerous honors: major showings of her graphics, drawings, and sculptures in great museums and galleries; handsome catalogues
and commentaries; critical articles and books; volumes of letters, diaries,
reminiscences, and other memorabilia.

Most of the material is in German. This book, though brief, is the first rounded summary in English of her life and art. The artist herself was largely indifferent to academic and professional art criticism. She cared more about the value of her work to people in general, especially those whose need for help so stirred her. She might well have found many art styles of the 1960s or 1970s obscure or inimical to her own taste, but she probably would not have been disappointed by the fate of her own surviving works. They have continued to be effective past her own time on earth.

A British art critic, Jaschia Reichardt, in a recent survey of art produced in the German Democratic Republic (East Germany) referred to Käthe Kollwitz as ". . . perhaps the most relevant source . . ." for an understanding of its development. This continuing influence derives indeed from Kollwitz's ". . . sensitive interpretation of the underprivileged."

Several artists active and officially esteemed in the German Democratic Republic are likened to Kollwitz in that they ". . . concentrate on the theme of the anguished human image." These include Lea Grundig, Hans Theo Richter, and Herbert Sandberg. Like Kollwitz before her, Lea Grundig was honored with the title of Professor. So, too, was Elizabeth Voigt, another graphic artist, once a master student with Kollwitz in Berlin.

Again and again the continuing importance of Käthe Kollwitz is demonstrated far and near. A distinguished art writer, Carl Zigrosser, whose book on the artist first appeared in the United States in 1951, wrote for a revised edition in 1969 that her voice ". . . still speaks to us with wisdom and compassion in these troubled times."

No survey of the greatest graphic work of the late nineteenth and first half of the twentieth century can be considered complete or representative without including many of her etchings, lithographs, and woodcuts. Her drawings often seem even more sensitive and spontaneous than her graphic work. And the sculptures she did in later life are more and more cherished. Not one is cold, formalistic, unfeeling, shallowly facile, or pretentious. Each is a direct, eloquent utterance in the authentic voice of a woman whose life and art were inseparably merged.

She once wrote of her hopes for her works after she herself was dead. If, decades later, they continued to exercise the effect she had intended— ". . . yes, then I shall have attained a great deal. For then people will have been enriched by me. Then I shall have been a co-worker in the great upbuilding."

The "Mourning Parents" share their silent, stone grief for the dead of both World Wars. These duplicates of the war-memorial statues for the soldiers' cemetery in Belgium have been erected in the ruins of this church at Cologne, beside the Rhine River.
Tourist Bureau, City of Cologne.

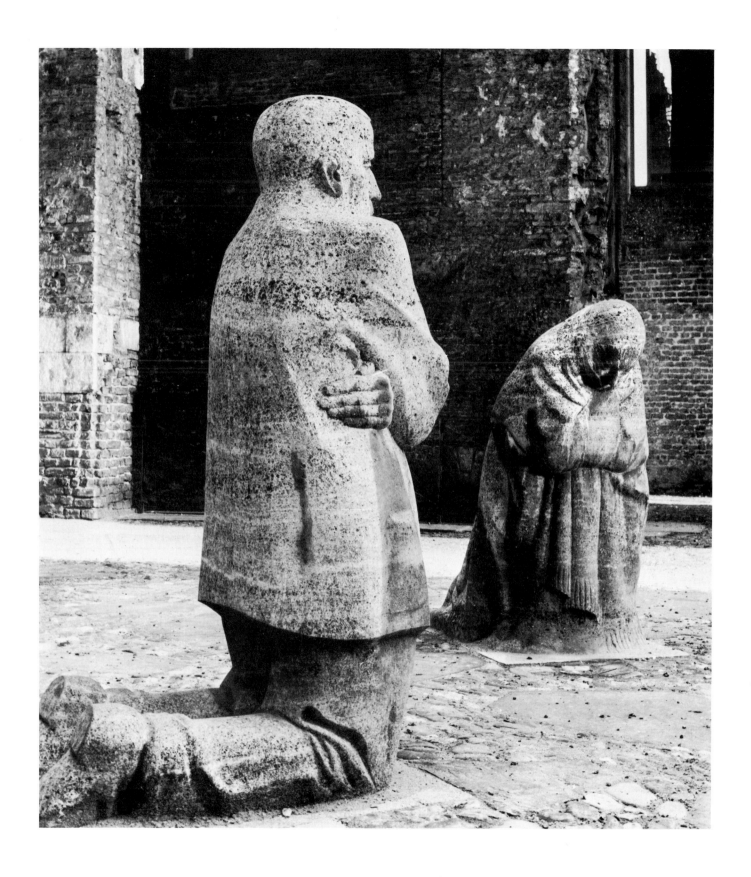

SELECTED BIBLIOGRAPHY

BITTNER, HERBERT. *Kaethe Kollwitz Drawings*. Reprint. New York: A. S. Barnes, 1959. 35 pp. + 147 illus.

BONUS-JEEP, BEATE. *Sechzig Jahre Freundschaft mit Käthe Kollwitz* [Sixty Years of Friendship with Käthe Kollwitz]. Boppard, Germany: Karl Rauch Verlag, 1948. 314 pp.

FANNING, ROBERT JOSEPH. *Kaethe Kollwitz*. Karlsruhe, Germany; New York: George Wittenborn, 1956. 137 pp.

KLIPSTEIN, AUGUST. *Käthe Kollwitz; Verzeichnis des graphischen Werkes* [The Graphic Work of Kaethe Kollwitz]. Bern: Klipstein & Co.; New York: Galerie St. Etienne, 1955. xx + 360 pp., 277 illus. The complete analytic guide to all the artist's known graphic prints, listing and reproducing her etchings, lithographs, and woodcuts.

KOLLWITZ, HANS, ed. *Briefe der Freundschaft*. Munich: List Verlag, 1966. 190 pp., 10 illus.

———— *The Diaries and Letters of Kaethe Kollwitz*. Translated by Richard and Clara Winston. Chicago: Henry Regnery, 1955. 200 pp., 50 illus.

———— *Ich sah die Welt mit Liebevollen Blicken*. Hannover: Fackelträger-Verlag. 1968. 404 pp., 84 illus.

———— *Käthe Kollwitz: Das plastische Werk*. Hamburg: Wegner Verlag, 1967. A portfolio of photographs of the artist's sculptures.

KOLLWITZ, KÄTHE. *Aus meinem Leben*. Munich: List Verlag, 1958. 212 pp. (paperback)

———— *Twenty-One Late Drawings*. Boston: Boston Book & Art, 1970.

MC CAUSLAND, ELIZABETH. *Käthe Kollwitz: Ten Lithographs*. New York: Henry C. Kleeman, Curt Valentin, 1941. 4 pp. + 10 pp. illus.

NAGEL, OTTO. *Die Selbstbildnisse der Käthe Kollwitz*. Berlin: Henschelverlag, 1965. 52 pp., 112 illus. The complete cycle of the artist's self-portraits from 1885 to 1943.

———— *Käthe Kollwitz*. Translated by Stella Humphries. Greenwich, Conn.: New York Graphic Society, 1971, 258 pp., 251 illus.

NÜNDEL, HARRI. *Käthe Kollwitz*. Leipzig: Bibliographisches Institut, 1964. 92 pp., 90 illus.

SCHMALENBACH, FRITZ. *Käthe Kollwitz*. Königstein im Taunus, Germany: K. R. Langewiesche, 1965. 6 pp., 72 pp. illus.

SHIKES, RALPH E. *The Indignant Eye: The Artist as Social Critic in Prints and Drawings*. Boston: Beacon Press, 1969, pp. xxiv, 255–68, 273–4, 277, 286.

ZIGROSSER, CARL, ed. *Kaethe Kollwitz*. New York: Bittner, 1946. 21 pp., 70 illus.

———— *Prints and Drawings of Käthe Kollwitz*. 1951. Revised edition. New York: Dover Publications, 1969. xxxii + 72 pp., 83 illus. (paperback)

INDEX

ABOUT THE AUTHORS

As young Americans working and studying in Berlin during the early 1930s, Mina C. Klein and H. Arthur Klein were first stirred by Käthe Kollwitz's prints. Leaving Germany some time after the start of the Nazi regime, they brought their enthusiasm for this artist back to the United States. This book is the result of years of study on their part, of four separate trips to postwar Germany, and of research in many museums and libraries throughout Europe and the United States.

Among the authors' other collaborations are *Peter Bruegel the Elder: Artist of Abundance*, *Great Structures of the World*, *Temple Beyond Time*, *Israel: Land of the Jews*, and English translations of works by German caricaturist, Wilhelm Busch. Mr. Klein is also the author of *Graphic Worlds of Peter Bruegel the Elder* and the writer-producer of the art film, *Bruegel's Seven Deadly Sins*. Mr. and Mrs. Klein live and write in Malibu, California.

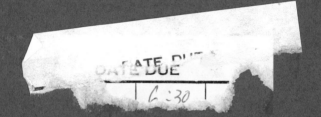